Fame Academy

The Book

Jordan Paramor

endemol u.k.

CONTENDER
BOOKS

WATCH OUT FOR FAME ACADEMY THE EXTENDED REMIX ON VIDEO AND DVD

Based on the Fame Academy programme produced for the BBC by Initial (part of Endemol UK Plc)

Executive Producer: Richard Hopkins
A special thanks to everyone on the production team who has helped with this project.

Fame Academy and the Fame Academy logo are trade marks of the British Broadcasting Corporation and are used under licence. Fame Academy © BBC 2002

BBC

BBC and the BBC logo are trade marks of the British Broadcasting Corporation and are used under licence. BBC logo © BBC 1996

First published 2002 by Contender Books
48 Margaret Street
London W1W 8SE
www.contendergroup.com/books

This edition published 2002
1 3 5 7 9 10 8 6 4 2

Text © Endemol UK, 2002

The moral right of Jordan Paramor to be identified as the author of this work has been asserted by her in accordance with the Copyright, Design and Patents Act, 1988.

I 1820366

ISBN 1 84357 045 9

All images supplied by BBC Picture Publicity and PA Photos, London

Project Co-ordination: Sasha Morton (Contender Books) and Frances Goddard (Endemol UK Plc)

Design by designsection, Frome, Somerset
Colour separations by Radstock Reproductions Limited, Midsomer Norton, Somerset
Printed and bound in Great Britain by Butler & Tanner Limited, Frome and London

BBC

Fame Academy

The Book

Jordan Paramor

Welcome to Fame Academy

FAME ACADEMY WAS ONE OF THE BIGGEST AND MOST EXCITING SHOWS OF 2002, WITH 12 TALENTED HAND-PICKED STUDENTS COMPETING ON THE BASIS OF THEIR VOCAL SKILLS AND SONGWRITING TALENTS TO WIN THE ULTIMATE PRIZE — THE LIFE OF A POP STAR FOR A YEAR.

Set in a £35 million mansion in London's exclusive Highgate, Fame Academy's mission was to teach the 12 students the skills they would need to make it big in the music business. Each student was picked for their drive, determination and, above all, their talent, from 36,000 18-35 year-olds who applied to attend the Academy.

In early 2002, budding pop stars were invited to either attend open auditions, or send off VHS tapes of themselves performing. Of the 10,000 who auditioned, just 20 hopefuls went through to the second round of auditions in London. From there, a very lucky 11 were chosen, while the twelfth and final student was selected by the public from three hopefuls during the first Live Showdown.

The chosen few had to attend several tough auditions, which featured singing tests and personality assessments. The judges also kept a close eye on the students at all times, to discover where their musical talents lay. Only those with the most potential were chosen.

The students lived in shared rooms in the Academy full time for up to ten weeks, and were filmed 24 hours a day by 35 eagle-eyed cameras and 70 microphones situated around the building.

The only places that were out of bounds to the cameras were the toilets, although recording did take place if they were used for anything other than their designated purpose – such as people trying to have private chats! Each morning the students were woken up at 6.30am from Sunday to Friday and at 9am on Saturdays by rousing Morning Songs, which blared from speakers around the Academy. Lights out was 11pm throughout the week, apart from after the Friday Night Live Showdown, when it was at midnight. A team of on-site caterers would prepare all meals to provide a nutritionally balanced diet. Each day the students were put through their paces during a strict daily timetable of lessons and training classes, which included vocal training, dance and songwriting classes. Three highly qualified teachers, a headmaster, and a personal development tutor were on hand at all times to guide the students through their stay.

On some days, time was set aside for the students to work on a Personal Development Programme (PDP), which involved group activities designed to test and develop qualities such as team skills and confidence. The students were also each given five minutes a day to write a daily journal on the computer in the Personal Tutor's room and were also required to do Web Chats – which they were told about the night before – in the Personal Tutor's Room before lessons.

Making The Grade

Every Monday morning the teachers and the Headmaster held a meeting in the Head's study to discuss the students' progress. After lengthy discussions, the three students whom the teachers felt had progressed least or been badly behaved were put on probation. Each Friday, the probationers had to Sing For Survival at the Live Showdown at Shepperton Studios, where the public had the chance to vote to keep their favourite probationer in the Academy. That student could return to the Academy and continue with their studies.

The remaining two probationers then had to face the Student Vote. Each student had the chance to save one of the remaining probationers by voting for the person they most wanted to stay in the Academy. The student with the least votes was then expelled. There was also a Grade A student every week, so-called because they had impressed the teachers throughout the week with their talent and attitude. Each Grade A student got a special reward – which could be anything from a designer hat to a ticket to a celebrity party. The Grade A student also got the opportunity to showcase their talents by performing a solo during Friday's Live Showdown.

Each student filled in a form prior to taking up their place at the Academy which required them to list their favourite songs including ones they would be happy to sing solo, their top Beatles

The Rules

There were certain rules that the students had to follow at all times. Richard Park kept a Rule Book where he logged all rule breaking or any arguments that took place between staff and students. Any students who broke the rules had to report to the Head and explain themselves. It was then up to him to decide on their punishments and hand out verbal or written warnings. Repeatedly bad behaviour or serious rule breaking could mean expulsion. The rules were as follows:

- The students had to wear their microphones at all times, except when taking a shower or sleeping.
- The students were not allowed to chew chewing gum.
- Alcohol was allowed at the discretion of the Headmaster, although it was not allowed in the students' rooms in any circumstance.
- The dance studio, recording studio, gym and offices were all locked from 8pm until 8am the following morning and were totally out of bounds to students.
- Musical instruments were not allowed to be played in the bedrooms, balcony, kitchenette, or bathroom.
- If students wanted to play instruments during the afternoon relaxation periods, up to three students could book half-hour sessions to practice in a designated area of the dance studio.
- Once a week the students were given the opportunity to perform one of their own songs during an acoustic session.
- After lights-out at 11pm, students were not allowed to turn the lights back on or to go outside the building into the Academy grounds. However, they were allowed on to the balcony adjoining the bedrooms.
- Students were never allowed into the recording studio or the Headteacher's office unless escorted by one of the teaching staff.
- Students were not allowed to move the furniture in the bedrooms, the living areas or the dining room.
- No smoking was allowed inside the Academy or on the balconies.
- Each student was allowed one phone call a week, the duration and time of which was decided by the Head. Each student got a choice of whom they wanted to speak to, but the final decision was down to the Head. During the phone call the students were banned from talking about how the show was being perceived by the outside world.
- Students were not allowed to engage in conversation with anyone else who entered the Academy, other than the students and teachers. Whenever students were outside the Academy grounds, they were briefed on the procedures to follow with people they met and talked to.
- The students were allowed to receive fan-mail, but it was vetted by the teachers before they were allowed to read it.
- At no time were the students allowed to discuss with students or teachers who they were planning to vote to save nor could they pass notes to each another.
- Students were expected to show respect to the Head and the teachers at all times. Insolence, rudeness and misbehaviour were not tolerated.
- Each student received a weekly allowance of £15, which could be spent on anything they needed in the Academy.

songs, tunes from the '60's, 70's etc and even their favourite songs from the movies. The Academy tutors would select songs from their list if they were singing for survival. Other solos and duets would be chosen for them. However, after some time in the Academy it would be expected that their vocals and image would evolve and they would need to update their lists.

The students were each allowed to take one suitcase each into the Academy. However, the following items were not allowed:

- No medical supplies
- No alcohol
- No illegal substances
- No weapons
- No money/cheque books/cards
- No books other than for religious requirements
- No mobile phones or pagers
- No palm pilots/electronic organisers or laptops
- No radios/personal stereos/ stereos or sound systems
- No cameras
- No items of clothing with prominent brands or commercial logos

- No pens/writing implements (any required were supplied)
- No writing paper/pads (any required were supplied)
- No diaries
- No professional photos
- No mirrors (including make-up mirrors)
- No hairdryers
- No candles
- No torches
- No chewing gum
- No more than two packets of 20 cigarettes
- No more than 5 personal photos

The Ultimate Prize

The pressure was on each and every one of the students throughout their stay in the Academy, as they knew that whoever won was in for the experience of a lifetime.

As well as getting an album deal with top music company Mercury Records, the winner would enjoy the use of an Audi TT sports car, a rent free luxury apartment in North West London, a session at the legendary Abbey Road Studios, a personal stylist, a cameo role in a movie, champagne on tap, flowers delivered every week and a holiday to The Caribbean on Concorde.

But there is one hitch: at midnight, exactly a year after they are handed their prize, it will be taken back. From then on the student – who is likely to have become a successful singer/songwriter – will have to fend completely for themselves!

This Old House

The Fame Academy mansion, the magnificent Witanhurst House in Highgate, is one of the most spectacular properties in Britain and the second largest privately owned stately home in London. It was specially converted for the show and boasted a dance studio, a gym, a recording studio, relaxation areas and even a hot tub. Neighbours of the incredible property include George Michael, Sting, Annie Lennox, Ringo Starr and Boy George.

The Grade 2 listed building is set in grounds of 5.5 acres and has 94 rooms, including more than 30 bedrooms. It has had many important visitors over the years; Queen Elizabeth II danced in the ballroom and master violinist Yehudi Menuhin played there. The mansion and its surrounding area has also had its fair share of uninvited guests over the years and is said to be home to several ghosts, including that of legendary highwayman Dick Turpin!

All in all, an amazing place for a group of potential superstars to be groomed for stardom!

Naomi Roper

DOB: 12/01/83
Star sign: Capricorn
From: The Scottish borders, now lives in London
Marital status: Single

The lowdown: Naomi is studying for a BA in acting at East 15 acting college in Essex. She is a huge motor racing fan and loves watching the Grand Prix. As well as her singing ambitions, she would love to make a film one day.

Showbiz background: Naomi taught herself to play rhythm guitar and can also play piano and violin. She writes her own songs, which she says are a mixture of folk, rock and indie.

Musical influences: Naomi's main musical influences are Kula Shaker, Captain Beefheart and his Magic Band, and Van Morrison. She also admires Jimi Hendrix for guitar, Keith Jarrett for piano and Nigel Kennedy for violin.

Ainslie Henderson

DOB: 28/1/79
Star sign: Aquarius
From: Denholm near Hawick, Scotland, now lives in London
Marital status: Has a long-term girlfriend

The lowdown: Ainslie landed a place at Edinburgh University after leaving school, but decided to defer his place for a year – five years ago! He taught himself to play the guitar and describes himself as a singer songwriter. He reckons his biggest achievement in life is playing a gig at the famous Viper Rooms in LA.

Showbiz background: After leaving school, Ainslie formed a band called Suburbia and landed a deal with City of Angels, a record company based in LA. Unfortunately the label went bust last year and Ainslie decided to move to London in search of fame and fortune!

Musical influences: The Beatles, Oasis, Radiohead, Jeff Buckley, Eric Clapton, Bjork and David Bowie. His favourite songwriter is Noel Gallagher.

Ashley House

DOB: 20/9/74
Star sign: Virgo
From: Cheltenham
Marital status: Married for three years

The lowdown: Before Fame Academy, Ashley taught Economics and Business at Cheltenham College. He also coached rugby, squash and cricket. He reads the Bible every morning to set himself up for the day and says he is entertaining, unpredictable and can get along with anyone.

Showbiz background: Ashley was a choirboy from the age of eight and plays trumpet, guitar and drums.

Musical influences: He loves all kinds of music except country and describes Corduroy, Queen and Montraux Alexander Trio as his biggest influences. Travis and Freddie Mercury are among his favourite songwriters.

Student Profiles

Sinead Quinn

DOB: 24/3/80
Star sign: Aries
From: Irvinestown, Ireland
Marital status: Single

The lowdown: Sinead has been singing since she was a young girl and her ambition is to leave her mark on the music industry in some way.

Showbiz background: Sinead recently graduated from the University of Hull in Music Technology. Before Fame Academy she made her money performing and working part time in a bar. She can play guitar, piano and mandolin and is a keen songwriter.

Musical influences: Sinead is inspired by anyone from Dolly Parton to Anastacia, with her favourite singer being Old Blue Eyes himself, Frank Sinatra. She also likes Paul Weller, Incubus, and rates Nickleback's 'How You Remind Me' as her favourite song of 2002.

Chris Manning

DOB: 23/12/78
Star sign: Capricorn
From: Poole in Dorset
Marital status: Single

The lowdown: Chris works part time in IT, and spends the rest of his time writing songs. He describes himself as romantic, respectful and tidy. He is also obsessed with Jackie Chan.

Showbiz background: Chris used to be in a boy/girl pop band, and is a bit of an all-rounder when it comes to showbiz. Not only would he like to crack the charts, but he's also a keen magician, would like to act in a serious major movie and would love to, erm, skydive.

Musical influences: Chris has eclectic musical tastes and is inspired by the likes of Frank Sinatra, Tom Jones and Robbie Williams. He is a big David Gray fan and songwriting wise he has a lot of respect for Paul Weller. Geri Haliwell and Ronan Keating, on the other hand, leave him cold.

David Sneddon

DOB: 15/9/78
Star sign: Virgo
From: Glasgow
Marital status: Has a long-term girlfriend

The lowdown: David plays in a band called The Martians and describes his job as 'singer in a pub band'. He enjoys playing 5-a-side football, watching movies, acting and playing video games.

Showbiz background: David is a self-taught pianist and also plays the drums. Fame Academy should be a doddle as he's no stranger to television, having been a presenter on a TV show called Inside Out in Aberdeen and Glasgow.

Musical influences: David's musical hero is Frank Sinatra, with his main influences being The Beatles, Van Morrison and Wet, Wet, Wet.

Katie Lewis

DOB: 5/5/84
Star sign: Taurus
From: Bristol
Marital status: Has a boyfriend

The lowdown: The youngest Fame Academy student loves drinking pints of cider and black, but hates animals and unhygienic people. Katie's plan is to be rich, famous, sing and be happy. In ten years she plans to have realised her dreams and be settled down and married.

Showbiz background: Katie has a BTEC in Performing Arts and is a classically trained singer. She belongs to the Starlight Dance and Theatre Club and has appeared in the the TV shows 'Casualty' and 'Teachers'.

Musical influences: Katie's favourite songwriter is Stephen Sondheim, while her biggest influences are Queen of Pop Madonna, Eva Cassidy and Celine Dion.

Marli [Marilena] Buck

DOB: 13/3/75
Star sign: Pisces
From: Lancashire, now lives in London
Marital status: Single

The lowdown: Marli works at the Florence Nightingale Hospital for Eating Disorders. Her aim is to be a successful singer songwriter, to make her own clothes and to help prevent bullying in schools. Her favourite party trick is wrapping her ankles around her neck whilst fire-breathing!

Showbiz background: Marli has already landed two record deals in the past, both of which fell through due to unfortunate circumstances. She plays the violin, clarinet, guitar and piano and is also a qualified piano teacher.

Musical influences: She is most influenced by Michael Jackson and Nik Kershaw and says that Madonna is her musical idol.

Malachi Cush

DOB: 23/9/80
Star sign: Virgo
From: Country Tyrone, Northern Ireland
Marital status: Single

The lowdown: Malachi comes from a very close-knit family who often stay up until the small hours singing and playing music. He had never left Ireland before the Fame Academy auditions and previously worked as a gas fitter.

Showbiz background: Malachi sang and performed at weddings from the age of three and was also in his school choir. Since he was 15 he has been heavily involved in charity work and raises money through his music.

Musical influences: Malachi enjoys all types of music, but mainly listened to folk whilst growing up. The three bands that have had the biggest influence on him are Van Morrison, U2 and The Pogues, with his favourite songwriter being Shane McGowan.

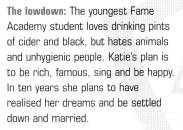

Lemar Obika

DOB: 4/4/78
Star sign: Aries
From: London
Marital status: Has a girlfriend of seven years

The lowdown: Lemar works as an Account Manager for a leading high street bank. He spends his spare time singing, going to the gym, writing songs and trying to teach himself piano. He is also a touch psychic, has a habit of talking to himself and boasts amazingly bendy thumbs!

Showbiz background: Lemar once had a record deal with RCA and has performed as a support act for various artists, including Destiny's Child.

Musical influences: Lemar favours soul, R'n'B, pop and garage, but hates heavy metal and cheesy pop. His favourite song is Boyz II Men's 'Mama'.

Nigel Wilson

DOB: 22/11/70
Star sign: Scorpio
From: Scunthorpe
Marital status: Married with four children

The lowdown: Nigel is a Vehicle Sales Manager in his native Scunthorpe. He enjoys watching videos, playing football, going to the gym, swimming, playing his guitar and songwriting. But his most important time is spent with his children.

Showbiz background: Nigel plays the guitar, drums, bass and a little of the keyboard. He has been singing and writing songs for years.

Musical influences: Nigel's dream is to sing with Robbie Williams and he is also a big fan of Aerosmith, Bryan Adams, Blue and Extreme. He likes all music, but favours a guitar-based sound.

Pippa Fulton

DOB: 26/6/82
Star sign: Cancer
From: Hull
Marital status: Has boyfriend of two years

The lowdown: Pippa is currently at stage school. She likes bowling, kick-boxing, going to the cinema, the film 'Alice In Wonderland', pubs, clubs and cartwheeling!

Showbiz background: Pippa has already had experience of playing in clubs, pubs and schools with her former bands, Wyke Street and Zulu.

Musical influences: Pippa loves r'n'b, pop and soft rock, especially Bon Jovi. She also rates Shaggy, Prince, Whitney Houston and loves Madonna.

Camilla Beeput

DOB: 9/9/81
Star sign: Virgo
From: North West London
Marital status: Single

The lowdown: Prior to Fame Academy, Camilla was working as a part time beauty consultant and was planning to go to Ealing Drama Studios in October. She enjoys reading plays and poetry and writes her own poems and songs. She's also kept a diary from the tender age of nine.

Showbiz background: Camilla taught herself piano and guitar and has had lessons in Contemporary and Hip Hop dance.

Musical influences: Camilla rates Blondie, TLC and The Gap Band as her biggest influences, and she admires Prince and Jimmy Hendrix. Her favourite songwriter is Marvin Gaye.

Tutor Profiles

Richard Park
Headteacher

There's no doubt Richard Park was the perfect candidate to become Fame Academy's Headteacher. Having spent more than 20 years at the forefront of British music, this is a man who knows more about the record industry than the artists themselves, making him the ideal person to lead the Fame Academy students in their quest for stardom.

Richard kicked off his showbiz career as a reporter on the Fife News, and he worked there for three years before scoring his first job in radio, as a presenter for both BBC Scotland and BBC Radio 1. From there he became presenter of music and sport at Radio Clyde, and in the mid-seventies he landed a column in the Scottish Daily Express, as well as a couple of presenting jobs on Scottish Television.

In 1979 Richard became Head of Entertainment and Sport at Radio Clyde where he won numerous awards, including Sony Broadcaster of the Year in 1983, Best Sport Presenter at the New York Radio Festival in 1984 and Scottish Radio and TV Programme of the Year in 1985.

However, Richard is best known for his work at Capital Radio between the years of 1987 and 1993, where he hired Pete Tong, Neil Fox, and Tim Westwood, amongst others. Whilst there he launched the first Help A London Child annual awards lunch and was appointed Director of Programmes for the Capital Gold Groups of stations in 1994.

Richard was made a fellow of the Radio Academy in 1993 and in 1994 was awarded the IMF British Music Roll of Honour for his outstanding contribution to British music. Between 1998 and 2001, he was also Chairman of the Prince's Trust 'Party In The Park' committee. Since 1996 Richard had been Director of Wildstar Records and was responsible for signing one of the biggest success stories of the past few years, Craig David, as well as many other British stars.

In 2001 he opened The Richard Park Consultancy, a cross-media company working with TV, Radio, Press, Advertising Agencies and the Music Industry. Richard is also the Chairman of the Anna designer fashion boutique chain.

Pam Sheyne
Songwriter

Pam Sheyne is a hugely successful songwriter and penned the massive hit 'Genie In a Bottle', which made Christina Aguilera a household name after it went to Number One in 27 territories. It also won Pam an Ivor Novello award for International Hit of the Year.

Pam also penned Billie Piper's Top 3 hit 'She Wants You', Jessica Simpson's U.S. smash 'Irresistible', and Dream's No.2 Billboard hit 'He Loves You Not'.

Pam has also worked with the likes of Eternal, Tina Arena, Kavana, CeCe Winans and Louise.

In addition, she is an accomplished guitarist, vocal producer and arranger and has performed backing vocals for such diverse artists as Lulu, Pet Shop Boys and Sisters of Mercy.

Jeremy Milnes
Personal Tutor

For over 25 years, Jeremy Milnes has been involved in teaching, acting and has worked as a learning mentor.

Jeremy's career began in 1979 after he graduated from the University of East Anglia. He worked with the British Council in Sri Lanka teaching drama and theatre to local teachers and, on returning to Britain, became Head of Drama at Willesden High School in North London. At the same time he auditioned for a series of acting jobs and joined the Molecule Theatre Company.

Jeremy has appeared in fringe theatre, touring theatre company productions and TV adverts all over the world. These include a French ad for Perrier directed by Ridley Scott, a German Bank advert with Rod Stewart's girlfriend Penny Lancaster, and for two years, Jeremy was 'Mr BMW' in a Spanish ad campaign.

Jeremy has also starred in the film 'Vapour Trail', appeared in TV shows 'The Bill' and '99-1' alongside Leslie Grantham, and co-presented the hugely successful BBC2 show 'Would Like To Meet'.

Most recently Jeremy trained as a Samaritan listener and has done a course in counselling skills. He has also been a learning mentor at Quintin Kynstan School in St John's Wood.

Jeremy lives in London and is divorced with three children.

Carrie Grant
Vocal Coach

During her time in the entertainment industry, Carrie Grant has been a recording artist, writer, dancer and presenter. She is also one of the best known and most respected vocal coaches in the music business, having worked with the likes of Will Young, Emma Bunton, Victoria Beckham, Melanie C, Take That, S Club, Charlotte Church and Atomic Kitten. She also recently produced the vocals on Atomic Kitten's Number One hit 'The Tide Is High'.

Carrie began her career as a dancer on TV shows, but swiftly moved on to presenting, fronting shows such as 'How Dare You', 'Freeze Frame' and the BBC's award-winning series 'Heart and Soul', on which she worked alongside her husband, successful recording artist David Grant.

From there Carrie moved on to session singing and worked with huge names like Diana Ross, Roberta Flack, Rod Stewart, The Lighthouse Family and Norman Cook.

During the late 90's Carrie and David were instrumental in forming the unique ten-piece multi-racial group United Colours of Sound and they remain members of the group to this day. As well as having their own successful recording career, United Colours of Sound have most recently featured on the Will Young single 'Evergreen'.

David and Carrie also worked together on the highly acclaimed gospel album 'Watching & Waiting' which won them a prestigious MOBO Award in 1998.

Carrie lives with David and their two children in North London.

Kevin Adams
Choreographer

Kevin Adams' range of dance styles includes Street, Ballet, Jazz, Tap, Locking, Body Popping, Breakdance, Ballroom, Salsa, Pas de Deux, Yoga, Aerobics, Personal Training and Contemporary, so it's hardly surprising that he's one of the most respected choreographers in Europe.

Over the last ten years he has been the UK and European aerobics champion, as well as being 4th in the world rankings. He has trained extensively with Paula Abdul in Los Angeles and worked with a truly extraordinary number of artists including Mariah Carey for her 'Honey' album launch, Cher for 'Strong Enough' and her BRIT Awards performance of 'Believe', Steps' sell-out 'Steptacular' Tour, Denise Van Outen for her 'Something For The Weekend' series, Louise for her 'Naked' video, Boyzone's 'Where We Belong' tour, The Spice Girls' BRIT Awards performance where Kevin appeared as a dancer and Eternal for performances at Party In The Park and the Smash Hits Poll Winners' Party.

Kevin worked with Helen Adams from Big Brother 2 on her fitness video and most recently he has been training and working with Jade Goody from Big Brother 3 on her fitness video.

Kevin lives in Essex with his fiancée and is soon to become a father for the first time.

Opening
Night

FAME ACADEMY'S FIRST TERM OFFICIALLY KICKS OFF ON
FRIDAY 4TH OCTOBER WITH THE STUDENTS BEING FLOWN
BY HELICOPTER TO SHEPPERTON STUDIOS FOR AN
ALL-SINGING, ALL-DANCING EXTRAVAGANZA TO INTRODUCE
THEM TO THE PUBLIC.

ELEVEN STUDENTS HAVE ALREADY WON A PLACE IN THE ACADEMY AND WITH ONE MORE PLACE TO BE WON, IT IS UP TO THREE HOPEFUL POTENTIAL STUDENTS TO TRY AND WIN THE PUBLIC VOTE AS THEY BATTLE IT OUT FOR THE FINAL PLACE.

In the studio the excitement is mounting and friends and family of the students have gathered to lend their support and wave banners and balloons. The live show begins at

8.30pm, introduced by TV favourites Cat Deeley and Patrick Kielty, who are dressed to impress and seem to be just as excited as the studio audience. The initial eleven students kick-off the proceedings by singing the Jackson 5's funky 'Can You Feel It', under the watchful eye of the Academy tutors. Then it's the turn of the three hopefuls to show what they can do.

Singing to get into the Academy are 24 year-old Glasgow native David Sneddon, who wows the crowd with his performance of Billy Joel's 'Uptown Girl'; 23 year-old Stoke-On-Trent lad Paul Macdonald, who does a strong rendition of Take That's 'Back For Good'. Finally 22 year-old Sinead Quinn from Northern Ireland blows everyone away with her version of Macy Gray's 'I Try'. The trio then have to wait until the second part of the show at 10.20pm to find out who will be gaining the coveted last place.

In the meantime the crowds are entertained by various smaller groups of the students, who have been well-rehearsed for the big night. Lemar, Katie, Camilla and Pippa strut through Destiny's Child's 'Say My Name', Naomi, Ainslie and Chris perform Toploader's anthem, 'Dancing In The Moonlight', and finally Malachi, Marli, Ashley and Nigel rock their way through T-Rex's classic 'Get It On'.

After some stomping performances, the eleven students flee back to the Academy by helicopter, while David, Paul and Sinead nervously await the results of the public vote. They even get the chance to have one last moment of glory as they

belt out a stomping version of 'You Can Go Your Own Way', by Fleetwood Mac.

There's a tense run-up while the votes are counted. David, Paul and Sinead line up on stage to wait for the result. There's clapping and cheering all around as Cat announces to an overcome Sinead that she will be taking the twelfth place in the Academy. "It's a bit weird, good weird. My heart's going!" Sinead says, looking flushed and sounding amazed.

Before she can say "I'm gonna be a star", Sinead sings her winning number one more time to a delighted audience, then waves goodbye to her friends and family and is making her way to the Academy on the back of a limo bike, trussed up in protective clothing and helmet over her glam evening outfit.

Meanwhile, the students who have already arrived at the Academy are amazed to get a

phone call from George Michael, who offers them words of support and encouragement for the next ten weeks. Not a bad way to start the term!

Accompanying Cat and Patrick at Shepperton Studios are the regular presenters of BBC Choice's Fame Academy coverage, who are always on hand to keep up to date with all the goings on. Vanessa and Danaan film their introductory links amongst the crowd before the show goes out live to the nation and are old hands at working with the audience to really get the excitement level building before the students take to the stage.

Vanessa Langford is a Showbiz Reporter for BBC's Liquid News and has travelled the globe from LA to Venice reporting on glamorous stories from the entertainment world. She spent a year as a Producer on Channel 5 News and as Showbiz Reporter and Editor for

ITN Radio, covering major events from the Oscars to the Brits and the Cannes Film Festival. Vanessa was also the voice of the BAFTA's and in 2002 and the host of her own show, 'Entertainment Weekend'.

Danaan Breathnach is the second BBC Choice presenter and also has a wide renging background in the entertainment industry. Having studied at Gaiety School of Acting, Danaan became a well known personality in Ireland, presenting several shows for RTE Network 2 including the 2000 Telethon for RTE. Danaan has worked as trainee Assistant Director on Mel Gibson's movie, Braveheart, and most recently presented 'Pop Will Shoot Itself' for Play UK and hosted the popular afternoon music show 'Select' for MTV UK and Ireland.

Interview

Jo

SHE'S THE UNSUNG HERO OF FAME ACADEMY, AND MUSIC MAESTRO JO IS HELPING THE STUDENTS TO COME ON IN LEAPS AND BOUNDS.

Who have you enjoyed working with?

I've been teaching Lemar, Katie, Camilla, Pippa and Naomi how to read music and I've been sneaking in time to help David out with his piano playing. He plays brilliantly, he just needs some help in certain areas. I've also been working with Marli on her piano playing.

Who do you think has progressed the most musically?

I think Pippa probably because she's found a whole new area of her voice that she didn't know was there. Camilla and Lemar are doing really well with their songwriting as well. They're all working hard and really coming on, but for some it's literally life changing.

Who do you think has the best chance of winning?

Ainslie is a strong contender and Lemar is obviously, but I think Sinead and Marli are up there as well. They're my top four.

Who have you had to be strictest with?

Nigel, definitely. I love him to death, but he seems to think because he's older he's a bit different to everyone else when it comes to learning so I'm always having to hassle him. Once he was on probation he really developed, learnt brilliantly for a week and a half, then slipped back into his "I'm too old for this" mode.

Which student has surprised you most?

David's songwriting ability and piano playing were a bit of a shock. He kept it all quiet and when we heard his stuff, it was just amazing.

Who do you think is being themselves and who is playing up to the cameras?

Ainslie is obviously playing up to the cameras and he's hilarious. I think some people are playing a very clever game and they're manipulating things emotionally in their favour. Well, they think it's in their favour but the teachers are one step ahead.

When do you think the tactical voting will begin?

I think the whole thing of chucking out the competition will really sink in the less people there are in the Academy.

Who do you think we'll see the biggest change in at the end of the competition?

David, probably. I'm hoping to see a bit more of Sinead's songwriting because she's got quite an interesting edge. Malachi I'm not sure about, but I'd like him to really develop and for all of us to go "Wow!" But I'm not sure that's going to happen.

Which student do you think will never give up on their dreams of fame?

Ainslie, and I don't think Sinead will. I think Sinead is very sure of who she is and where she wants to go. Regardless of the outcome of Fame Academy she will be still be doing her thing. I think Marli definitely has something going on and she will stick to it, but I think it's all very emotional for her and she has to be careful. I think overall there's a huge amount of talent in the Academy and some of the students can – and hopefully will – go on to do amazingly well.

Week One

IT'S THE DAY AFTER
THE FIRST LIVE SHOW
IN WHICH TALENTED
IRISH SINGER/
SONGWRITER SINEAD
WON THE LAST PLACE
IN THE ACADEMY AND
ALL OF THE STUDENTS
ARE BUSY ADJUSTING
TO LIFE INSIDE THE
£35 MILLION MANSION

Saturday

On their first day at the Fame Academy all of the students are busy adjusting to life inside the £35 million mansion. They will soon have to get used to being filmed by super-sensitive cameras 24/7, waking at 6.30am to thumping music for a tough days' lessons and to Headmaster Richard Park's booming voice following them around throughout their stay.

After getting up at the leisurely time of 9am to the strains of Wham's 'Wake Me Up Before You Go Go', the guys and girls spend their first official day at the Academy doing a full timetable. They also watch the previous night's performances and are all visibly shocked at how badly they came across onscreen. It's no wonder Richard tells them "Every moment in here will be valuable." It seems the students are beginning to realise just what this means.

Later in the day all the teachers agree that there's a lot of work ahead of them. "My mark of 15 out of 100 for a BBC live performance on a Friday night is not acceptable," says Richard.

During an acoustic jamming session in the reception, Ashley's confidence is crushed when he hears Lemar sing Boyz II Men's 'Water Runs Dry' perfectly. He is comforted by Nigel who's also having an attack of insecurity.

That evening the students discuss the day and are also introduced to Richard's Little Black Book, in which he will be writing down a list of all the rule breakers. He will also be using red and yellow cards to dish out discipline. "I want to keep a nice tight ship… The more we can follow a set of codes, the better it can be."

Later in the evening personal tutor Jeremy introduces the students to a fun question and answer game during their Personal Development Period (PDP). Jeremy explains to them that, "It's fun, but there's a serious side to it. It's really important you begin to work as a group and trust each other."

During the game Ainslie says he thinks his girlfriend is "the one", Sinead admits to having snogged a girl, Naomi confesses she's had sex in a Jacuzzi, Katie says the thing she would most like to change about herself is her boobs and Marli confesses that if she had to be marooned on a desert Island with anyone from the group, it would be Ainslie because: "He makes me giggle and he's cute to look at!"

The evening is rounded off with a rousing pillow fight, which Ainslie seems to enjoy more than anyone.

Sunday

After being woken up at the crack of dawn, the weary students have their first choreography lesson with Kevin. He doesn't think they're ready to practise the song he had in mind for them: "Until we feel that everyone is up to speed and can handle the big opening, the big numbers in between, and the big closing, we will not be doing it."

Thankfully Kevin is more impressed with the students once the class gets going, and there are even a few whoops of joy at the end of the lesson. But as the other students skip off to lunch. Malachi stays behind to ask for some extra help from Kevin.

In the afternoon everyone has a private singing lesson with Carrie. It is good news for Camilla who was told that her voice is "beautiful" and "magical". But bad news for Ainslie who was so busy strumming on his guitar that he missed his lesson, leading to a grovelling apology to Carrie. Despite this, he was soon in trouble again when all the students were 15 minutes late for their singing lesson: "Ainslie it's inexcusable. You missed my lesson. You're the last person into the ensemble, it's unacceptable," Carrie tells him.

That evening Richard warns the students that if these problems continue he will start dishing out punishments. Ainslie is less than impressed with the pep talk. "I feel it should be a show about musicians and talent, not about people pretending to be in some little school. I think that's pathetic," he rants.

And it is Katie's turn to rant later on when she tells the girls she feels that Nigel is patronising towards her. Tensions are mounting...

Monday

For the first time, the mentors meet in Richard's office to decide which students will be put on probation this week. They decide on Pippa, Ashley and Nigel, who will be 'Singing for Survival' on Friday's show. Marli is named as the Grade A student with all the teachers' agreeing she has worked consistently hard in all of her lessons. "She is focused on the goals of the Academy," Richard tells the clapping students when the announcements are made in the dance studio later in the day. Naturally, those on probation are less than happy; Nigel holds his hands in front of his face, a crying Pippa is comforted by Marli and Ashley looks shell-shocked, later shedding a few tears.

Ainslie is called to the Headmaster's office later in the afternoon after his sneaky cigarette on the balcony the night before is discovered. "If you let somebody get on with their own whims, at the expense of others, then we're going to make for a very unhappy camp," Richard tells him. "The weather is changing and people's voices are too If you smoke near them and mess up their voices, they will not be happy with you at all."

In fact it seems that there is already trouble in the voice department, with Naomi and Sinead complaining of sore throats, Marli suffering from migraines and not only has Lemar been stung by a wasp, he also has a niggling cough. Oh dear.

Marli and Camilla comfort Pippa as she tearfully tells them she wants to get better, and aspires to be like Geri Halliwell because she "never gives up". Nigel tells Lemar being on probation is making him feel up and down, while a despondent Ashley suffers from a lack of confidence and tells Malachi, "I'm a teacher, so no one likes teachers. No one likes people with privileged upbringings. No one likes Christians. I'm stuffed. I'm old."

"You're an ancient Christian teaching freak!" Malachi laughs, trying to cheer him up.

All the students perk up that night when they are awarded free time, and given Zoolander to watch on DVD. Ainslie, accompanied by Malachi and Naomi chill out together singing U2 songs.

Tuesday

The students are treated to a luxury lie-in and don't have to get up until the luxury time of 7.15. At their early morning dance class they are less than impressed at being given a pair of ballet shoes each, while Kevin is even less impressed with Camilla being six minutes late and tells her: "This really isn't good enough. This isn't the first time this has happened and we need to rectify it."

After the two and a half-hour choreography session, Camilla gets to work out her frustration on the punch bag in the gym. Meanwhile, Katie and Chris practise the dance routine for their duet on Friday's live show, followed by Malachi and Sinead who are also keen to perfect their routine.

After lunch, Marli heads for her room looking upset, and a concerned Ainslie follows her to make sure she's okay. "I listened to my vocal back and I was really embarrassed. I shouldn't be a Grade A student, I don't deserve it. I don't see that I've got my own style. Here, I feel really lost," she tells him sadly.

"You're Marli. You have to come to terms with being fabulous and learn to care a little less," comes the caring chap's reply.

At a teachers' meeting a concerned Carrie suggests that Naomi should see a vocal specialist as soon as possible as she keeps losing her voice. There's also some criticism for Nigel who Pam describes as: "Mr Angry and Upset. He doesn't take to listening to you."

Poor Katie has a confidence crisis and is found sobbing in the kitchen. "I just feel so crap," she sniffs. There are comforting words from Camilla who tells her: "Don't ever think that you're not good. It's not that you can't sing is it?" While Pippa adds: "Look at the state of me yesterday, I didn't stop crying. I had no confidence, and now I'm thinking that maybe I've been put on probation to give me confidence".

The mood is lightened when Richard announces that Marli is to be given a hat from top designer Philip Treacy for being the Grade A student and Pippa is relieved that Richard has taken pity on her, so she will be allowed to get her roots done.

Over dinner, Marli confides that she once had a record deal worth £1/2million, but the deal fell through and she spent the £150,000 advance on building her own recording studio. "Do you know how many people get signed and get their record on the shelves?" she asks.

A session with the Academy's personal stylist that evening cheers Katie up no end, while Jeremy encourages the students to start the Academy's first Yearbook. "You can talk about friendships, rivalries and what you know about each other at the moment. Make it as picturesque and colourful and bright and imaginative and creative as possible," Jeremy tells them. So far the book records that Naomi is most likely to fall in love with someone in the Academy, Marli is the most likely to own her own record company and Katie is most likely to cry or fart!

thigh so gets a piggyback into the Academy from Kevin.

Richard and Kevin meet to discuss Naomi, who will be seeing a throat specialist later that day. Richard voices concerns about Ashley and Nigel's performances, but is reassured that they are coming on in leaps and bounds. He is still nervous about Friday's live show, though: "Friday night will be the biggest test this Academy has ever had," he tells Kevin.

Nigel is now feeling pretty confident, and despite admitting to feeling a bit out of it as the oldest student, he is buzzing as he talks about his fellow probationers. "Pippa, I think, has nothing to worry about. She's coping very well. Ashley is strong as an ox. He's just getting on with life." Time will tell...

Come the evening, Naomi is gutted after discovering that she won't be singing on Friday. The vocal therapist thinks that it's likely to be cysts or nodules causing her problems and she is devastated. Everyone rallies around her to support her as they hear that her condition is to be monitored over the weekend, but sadly if it doesn't improve, she may be forced to leave the Academy.

Spirits are lifted when Jeremy introduces a new game to the students where they have to write 100 words about another student. Their scribblings are then read out, while everyone else has to guess who they're describing.

MARLI

SHE'S A LEADER AND A SHINING EXAMPLE. SHE WAS LEADING THE GROUP
THE TEACHERS

I'M VERY IMPRESSED WITH HER. SHE'S GREAT. SHE'S HUNGRY FOR IT. SHE'S A WORKER
THE TEACHERS

IT'S UNANIMOUS, AND THAT'S A WORD WE PROBABLY WON'T BE HEARING AGAIN
RICHARD

GRADE A

"FRIDAY NIGHT WILL BE THE BIGGEST TEST THIS ACADEMY HAS EVER HAD" RICHARD

However, the real secrets of the book won't be discovered until November, as it will be locked up in the Head's office for the next five weeks.

wednesday

Kevin's morning warm up involves an outdoor relay race of boys versus girls. The girls are victorious, but poor Marli slips and injures her

Pippa is the first to read hers out: "I'm a person who is very sure of who I am... I enjoy myself to the full, I don't give a damn what others think, I am a leader not a follower," she proclaims. The others rightly guess she is being Ainslie and the game continues successfully. With spirits still high, Malachi, Ainslie, Naomi and Lemar decide to play a trick on Chris and smear chocolate in his pants. But will he get the gag?!

Thursday

Katie and Chris start the day rehearsing Shanice's 'I Love Your Smile' for Friday night's live final. Katie grins widely when Carrie tells her: "You sound fab. You just have to get your timing. You've got the most amazing soul tone, with classical timing. We need to give you soul timing. Instantly. Now."

Although Chris needs to brush up in parts, Carrie encourages him, with "Timing was gorgeous, and tone was gorgeous."

The work that the probationers are putting into their songs for the live final is paying off and Carrie tells Pippa: "There's been a transformation in this lady this week. That was amazing. You are singing in your voice and not someone else's. This is the real Pippa. You look absolutely stunning. You're very talented. I want you to believe that." Pippa wipes away a few tears before telling Marli that

it is the nicest thing anyone has ever said to her.

Later that evening, the probationers are given the chance to convince the other students that they should vote to keep them in the Academy. They have just one minute to give their speech and then they all must go and pack their suitcases just in case they are expelled.

Pippa tells the group, "I do have something special and I am lucky. Since I've met you you've made me realise what music is all about."

Nigel announces that: "The last days I've spent with you guys have obviously been a pleasure for me. I love you all and I've loved spending time with you."

Then it was Ashley's turn. "If I was watching tomorrow night I hope I'd see a teacher who's given up things to chase things he's always wanted. So if I can get a nurse, or a bin man, or someone who works in a shop to go for it... that's what I want."

It seems the pressure won't only be on the probationers tomorrow night...

Friday

The day of the live showdown dawns and the tension is showing. All three students who are on probation are feeling the pressure and know that if they don't put in a good performance tonight, they may not return to the Academy.

Naomi is miserable as she can't sing during the show because of her throat problems and Carrie is also feeling nervous after the first week of vocal training. "That was, categorically, one of the worst performances I've ever seen on television," she tells the students after watching the first week's show. Let's hope things improve tonight!

NIGEL HE HAS TO REVEAL THAT EXTRA SOMETHING TO GO TO THE TOP AND BE A STAR IN THE ACADEMY. GET DOWN TO IT FROM THIS POINT ON, BUT TRY TO RELAX A LITTLE AS WELL
RICHARD

PIPPA BEGINNING TO DEVELOP, BUT NOT QUITE THERE
RICHARD

ASHLEY YOU HAVE TRIED TO GIVE IT EVERYTHING BUT WE DETECT A PROBLEM WITH CONFIDENCE
RICHARD

ON PROBATION

week one

DOWN AT SHEPPERTON STUDIOS THE ATMOSPHERE IS A MIXTURE OF NERVES AND EXCITEMENT, WITH PRESENTERS CAT AND PATRICK COMING CLOSE TO BEING THE MOST NERVOUS OF EVERYONE. "MOTHER OF SWEET JESUS, I'M S****ING MYSELF," PATRICK TELLS THE AUDIENCE, WHILE CAT NODS ANXIOUSLY IN AGREEMENT.

Once again the audience is filled with the students' supporters, but it's the viewers at home that the probationers really have to impress.

First up is Nigel who belts out the Wilson Pickett classic 'In The Midnight Hour', as the Head pats his knee and sings along. Next up, Pippa sings Nelly Furtardo's 'I'm Like a Bird'. Jeremy sings along and looks delighted with her performance. Finally it's Ashley's turn, and he smiles nervously before bursting into Otis Redding's 'I Can See Clearly Now'. When Ashley finishes he joins the rest of the students for a group hug and then the long wait for the results begins.

While the votes start flooding in, the other students take the opportunity to show the audiences what they can do. Sinead and Malachi go first and perform Bryan Adams and Mel C's 'When You're Gone', Marli gets to sing on her own as part of her prize for being Grade A student and performs Natalie Imbruglia's 'Torn' with Naomi accompanying her on guitar. Ashley, Lemar and Camilla are next up singing U2's 'Pride (In The Name Of Love)', and Katie and Chris duet on Shanice's 'I Love Your Smile'.

After the performances the teachers are asked who they thought performed best and all agree that Lemar was the real show-stopper. But the studio audience don't agree and boo when Lemar's name is announced. Hmmm, a bit of sour grapes from the other students' supporters, perchance? After a tense wait, Cat and Patrick join the three probationers on stage to announce who is safe and which two probationers will be put to the student vote. Nigel is ecstatic when he is told that he is safe with 41% of the public vote, so its now up to the students to decide if Pippa or Ashley will stay on. They all

who voted for who?

CHRIS ▸ PIPPA
SINEAD ▸ PIPPA
LEMAR ▸ PIPPA
AINSLIE ▸ ASHLEY
MARLI ▸ PIPPA
MALACHI ▸ PIPPA
NAOMI ▸ PIPPA
CAMILLA ▸ PIPPA
KATIE ▸ PIPPA
NIGEL ▸ ASHLEY

take their places on lit-up stools and cast their votes by writing their chosen student down on a board. Then one by one, they reveal who they have selected. Ashley and Pippa huddle together as the names are read out, but it's soon obvious that it's bye bye to Ashley as he takes only two votes to Pippa's eight.

He takes it in good spirits and wishes them all well "Good luck guys, you've been brilliant" before the whole group perform 'Lean On Me'.

See ya, Ashley, you'll be missed.

Interview
Ashley

HE'S THE FIRST OUT, AND ASHLEY WANTS TO HAVE HIS SAY! THE FORMER TEACHER REVEALS HE RECKONS LEMAR COULD WIN, KATIE OR PIPPA WILL BE NEXT OUT, AND WHY RICHARD PARK COULD NEVER CUT IT AS A REAL TEACHER.

How do you feel about being the first out of Fame Academy?

I'm obviously disappointed because you don't go into it to be chucked out first. It's been a great experience and I don't regret anything.

Did you have any idea you were going to go in the first week?

Obviously you know when you're on probation one of you is going to go, but I didn't think it would be me. I honestly didn't expect the public to vote for Nigel. I think if it had been between me and Nigel for the student vote, no-one would have voted for Nigel. Somebody told me they thought Nigel got the chip-shop vote. Everyone north of wherever would have voted for him because he's a truck salesman, he's got four kids, he's 31 and he's also a lovely guy. Whereas the people who would have voted for me were probably at dinner parties.

Are you annoyed with the students who didn't vote for you?

I was disappointed with two people who didn't vote for me – Malachi and Naomi. I knew Ainslie would vote for me because he's a top guy, and I knew Nigel would. I also thought Malachi would have done, but he voted on the performance on the night. I know he cried all the way home on the bus. I also thought Marli would have voted for me as she said earlier in the week I had nothing to worry about.

Were you pleased with your performance?

With most of it, yes. But there was a bum note at the end.

What did you think of Nigel and Pippa's performances?

Brilliant. They were both fantastic. Both of their performances were better than mine.

How did you feel when you first found out you were up for expulsion?

I was more worried about Nigel and Pippa, really. I knew that Pippa would be upset and I also knew Nigel would be because he didn't feel like he was part of the group. People in the group have some issues with him.

The teachers said you lacked confidence and energy. Do you agree?

I don't lack confidence in myself as a person, but I don't think I was as good as other people in the Academy. Some of them have had record contracts before and I knew I wasn't the best vocalist there. But I knew that I could have developed into one of the best performers there. As for the lack of energy? That's rubbish.

What were your best experiences in the Academy?

My conversations with Malachi and Ainslie. And it's cool when the teachers praise you.

And the worst?

When it was announced that I was on probation and Richard Park gave the reasons. That made

me angry because he doesn't know me and yet he felt able to comment on my personality.

How did you get on with the other teachers?
Kevin is a legend, but he was so harsh and strict with us. But he made sure none of us mucked about in his classes! I think he took a shine to me and was genuinely sad to see me go. Carrie was a great vocal coach, but I was disappointed she didn't stick up for me more. Jeremy was lovely. He was always willing to help, but he knew when not to be around.

As a teacher yourself, which of the teachers do you think would cut it in a real school environment?
Kevin definitely could, Carrie probably could, Pam I didn't see enough of to know and Jeremy used to be a teacher so he definitely could. Richard Park, definitely not! Not a chance. He's got a job to do and he's doing it, but I don't think he'd last as a real teacher.

Who did you become close to during your time in the Academy?
I've been close with Nigel since the auditions. I became close to Malachi very quickly as well and I also got on well with Ainslie and Naomi.

What and who did you miss?
I missed my wife Jay, obviously, and I missed school and my pupils.

But you're not going back to your school, are you?
No, I had to resign. I wouldn't change anything, though. I would do it all again.

What are you planning to do now?
I'll wait and see. I'd love to be a TV or radio presenter. Of course I would love to sing as well, but my guess is that probably won't happen as I'm the first one out.

Who do you think has a good chance of winning Fame Academy?
Lemar or Marli. I think all of us think Lemar is going to win. But you never know what the public think. Since I've been out people have said they don't understand why Chris wasn't on probation, whereas we thought he had the third best chance of winning. Ainslie could win or he could go next week, because he's a rock star who finds it hard to hit some notes.

Who do you think will be up for probation next week?
Chris and Ainslie, and Pippa or Katie. I think Katie or Pippa could go.

Do you think you would have suited the pop star lifestyle?
Yes, but I would never have become a precious diva. I would have liked to make people feel good when I was performing. And I would also like to inspire people to go for their dreams.

week Two

FOLLOWING ASHLEY'S EXPULSION, THE STUDENTS ARE IN SURPRISINGLY HIGH SPIRITS AND ARE WELCOMED BACK FROM SHEPPERTON STUDIOS ON FRIDAY NIGHT WITH A DRINK FROM THE HEADMASTER, TO CELEBRATE THE END OF THEIR FIRST WEEK

Saturday

Pippa and Nigel are incredibly relieved to have survived probation, while Ainslie sings a song for expelled Ashley.

Despite having had a steam treatment for her throat, Naomi is disappointed to be told that she won't be able to join rehearsals for the group song for the next live final. She is instructed to take loads of rest and goes off to bed. Later, she creeps on to the balcony to practise her singing while no one else is around. Tsk!

The students and teachers watch a video of the previous night's performances and are thankfully a bit happier than the previous week.

Carrie still isn't convinced about Malachi and Sinead's duet, saying: "I think I've heard it better." Richard also has his say: "The good news is that we're improving. The bad news is we've got a long way to go to get to the standard I've got in mind for you. It's back to the drawing board."

Ainslie makes Pam cry when he performs his self-penned track 'Don't Throw Your Love Away'. "That's beautiful," she sniffs. She also tells him: "I think you're one of the best songwriters here. You can be a leader and teach the others what you know."

The students have a sing-in in the lounge, impressing the Head no end. He describes Katie as having, "A voice reminiscent of a beautiful day in Bristol" and also heaps praise upon Lemar.

Ainslie and Katie instigate a chocolate mousse fight, then all the students play a game of truth led by Jeremy – and reveal some saucy secrets! A pillow fight in the boys' room follows before bedtime.

Sunday

The day kicks off with a pep talk from the Head who is irritated by some of the students' behaviour. Richard warns that rule breaking can count towards grading, but Ainslie is unhappy at being told what to do and tells a stony faced Richard: "I think that's really ludicrous. I think it should be on how hard you work in the lessons."

In Kevin's session, the trainer is unimpressed by Malachi's efforts, Sinead is struggling, Naomi is told to work harder and Katie is named teacher's pet. Lemar and Camilla pick up the dance moves easily, whilst Nigel has come on leaps and bounds with the help of Lemar.

During her vocal class Katie picks up some top tips from Carrie. "You have so much potential. You've just got to believe in yourself. I actually don't think you are slow at learning, I think you don't have the confidence."

Chris had a few problems during his individual singing class, but with Carrie's help, he's soon flying. During Ainslie's class, however, a worried Carrie asks him to tone down his bad behaviour. "I wanted to figure out how much misbehaving I could do before being put on probation for it," he smiles cheekily. Carrie repeats her plea and tells him she's only saying it because she thinks he's got an amazing talent.

There's bad news for Naomi later in the day when it is announced that she will be leaving the Academy the following morning, on the advice of voice specialists. "This is probably one of the hardest things I'm going to have to do here," Richard admits as he tells her fellow students. There are gasps all round, especially when Naomi emerges sobbing from the Personal Tutor room. "This so sucks," she tells the rest of the group as they take turns to hug her. "You'll get so many offers. You'll be brilliant!" Pippa tells her.

It seems Ainslie is hit the hardest by the news and he slinks off sadly. He tells Jeremy: "I'm so gutted. It's going to be so grey without Naomi," and later offers her a shoulder to cry on as she tearfully talks about life outside the Academy.

Monday

It's a sad start to the day as the students say an emotional goodbye to Naomi. The group have a quick singalong and goodbye hugs before Jeremy escorts her from the Academy. The group are soon brought back down to earth when Richard tells them: "As I said last night, this is a really, really sad moment but for the rest of us it's back to business as usual."

It certainly is. A three hour dance class follows, with Nigel once again showing he is finally getting the hang of Kevin's choreography, although Sinead still has some work to do.

Come lunchtime, it's bad news for Chris, Katie and Pippa who will all have to Sing for Survival on Friday night. Pippa and Katie are clearly upset, while Chris takes the news gracefully and nods in agreement when Richard says he has been "coasting along". However, there's great news for Lemar, who has been given the Grade A tag. He celebrates by picking a fight with a marble bust in the entrance hall. Hmm....

The reality of being on probation hits Chris later in the day and Sinead questions his quiet mood. "It's not probation that's put me down," he tells her, "It's having certain things pointed out to you. It's like therapy." He confesses that he's a lot more vulnerable than he seems and will make sure the real him comes to the fore if he stays in the Academy.

Malachi gets some extra dance lessons and Kevin offers some words of comfort to the struggling Irishman. "I've seen worse dancers than you in some good bands," he tells him, before adding, "There's never been a dancer like you. When they made you, they broke the mould."

The big news of the day is that 24 year-old David Sneddon, who was one of the three who sang for a place in the Academy during the very first show, will arrive tomorrow. But how will the other students react?

Tuesday

The day begins with a full-on exercise class in which Kevin pushes the students so hard they sweat buckets and Pippa injures her thigh. She is told by a physiotherapist that she has a slight tear in one of the quadriceps and will have to sit out the dance sessions for a couple of days to recover. Whoops.

Lemar is ecstatic when Richard tells him he will be attending the National TV Awards that night with Cat Deeley and Patrick Kielty as his reward for being Grade A student. "I'm feeling that, I'm feeling that!" he laughs before hugging the Head.

In a songwriting session with Pam three groups are formed and Sinead, Ainslie and Malachi soon came up with a fantastic number. Nigel, Pippa and Chris, and Camilla, Marli, Katie and Lemar's groups find things a tad harder.

The new student, David, arrives early in the afternoon and is welcomed by the rest of the group. Despite quizzing him about the show, they are disappointed when he tells them that he hasn't been watching it, and isn't allowed to tell them anything anyway!

The girls have a session with super-stylist Kirsty in preparation for Friday's live showdown. Lemar got smartened up and couldn't wait to hit the town with Carrie, Kevin, Cat and Patrick. He admits he's excited about the booze, but is told by a stern Kevin: "I'll be checking up on you. There will be no alcohol for you tonight!" Hmmm, we'll see.

The students who have been left behind get evening drinks as a treat to welcome David. Relaxing quickly into the group, David doesn't even raise an eyebrow when Ainslie and Malachi decide to dress up in some of the girls' clothes!

It soon becomes obvious that Kevin is unsuccessful with his plan for keeping Lemar away from the alcohol, and the poor chap arrives back from his night out looking a little unsteady on his feet!

CHRIS HAS BEEN COASTING ALONG, NEEDS TO FND HIS TRUE IDENTITY
RICHARD

PIPPA CAN GIVE SO MUCH MORE
RICHARD

KATIE HAS PROBLEMS WITH TIMING AND RHYTHM
RICHARD

ON PROBATION

WEEK TWO

Wednesday

Arriving six minutes late for the lesson, Lemar initially struggles through Kevin's dance class after his night on the tiles, but he quickly perks up and proves the show must go on by dancing like a pro.

Richard and Jeremy have a chat about the probationers and Jeremy admits that he has some concerns about Chris's abilities, although he's feeling more confident about Katie and Pippa.

Marli and Ainslie practise their raunchy dance routine for their duet on Friday night. Kevin tells them he wants to see "sex, glamour… everything that's missing from my life." Poor bloke!

In a showcase of the songs they have written, Richard and Pam are impressed with Ainslie, Malachi and Sinead's track, 'Making Me Mad', and also heap praise on the other songs, 'Get To Where You Are' and 'Watching Me'. As the students go to lunch, Richard is confident that 'Making Me Mad' could be a smash hit and suggests to Pam that the Group go into the studio to record it.

After an unsuccessful session with the stylist, Kirsty, yesterday, Sinead is feeling a bit insecure, and gets some welcome attention from Kevin who tells her he is going to devise a workout for her to help her to feel better about her body. Sinead is pleased, although a bit concerned that the workout will give her big muscles!

Wednesday night is full of drama as the students play another rousing game of Truth Or Dare. the Academy sees its first proper snog after Ainslie dares Chris and Marli to French kiss for a full 30 seconds. Other dares see Katie kissing David's nipple, and Camilla attempting to wake a sleeping Lemar up with a kiss. Things are certainly hotting up in Jeremy's sessions…

Thursday

The teachers gather to discuss the students who are Singing for Survival. Carrie's money is on Katie going, Richard thinks Chris will walk, while Kevin refuses to name names, and instead refers to their original meeting where he suggested that Camilla should be put on probation.

Ainslie had to go for an X-ray as it was thought he could have cracked some ribs after his wrestling match with Malachi. The Headmaster pretends to Malachi that he has broken two bones and a panic-stricken Malachi is relieved when the joke is revealed and it turns out that Ainslie just has bruised, not broken, ribs. Who says Richard doesn't have a sense of humour?

Having already been on probation the week before, Pippa is well equipped to offer Katie some advice for Friday night: "Everyone's on your side. Everyone cheers, and they're cheering for you. The worst bit is at the end when you're waiting for the votes and stuff. Whatever will be will be," she tells a terrified Katie.

The time comes for the students to make their heartfelt plea to keep them in the Academy. Chris spent his minute singing a specially written number called, ironically, Save Me: "Save me 'cos I'm a guy who doesn't boast... much. And if you save me I'll make you wicked cheese on toast."

Katie sheds a few tears as she tells the group: "The last couple of weeks have been like a dream come true. You're all the best. Whatever happens tomorrow I already feel like a winner." Next up is old pro Pippa who jokes: "If anyone ever needs any counselling in probation you know where to come because I'm quite experienced. I've been in the business now for quite a while!"

Chris, Malachi and Ainslie find it hard to settle down to bed and take a stroll in the grounds before heading noisily back to their bedroom and waking Lemar and Nigel.

Ainslie gets a surprise when Chris jumps out at him from behind a curtain, while Malachi hides by the side of his bed and leaps on him. No wonder the poor boy can't sleep!

Friday

The students start the day by rehearsing tonight's live showdown and then they all head down to Shepperton Studios to have a final run-through and get themselves dressed up and looking gorgeous. Before they know it, it's time to face the public once again...

LEMAR

QUIETLY CONFIDENT
AND VERY SURE
OF HIMSELF
THE TEACHERS

GRADE A

Sing for Survival

IT'S SHOW TIME AND AS USUAL THE STUDENTS' SUPPORTERS ARE OUT IN FORCE, ADDING TO THEIR ALREADY JANGLING NERVES.

Pippa is the first of the probationers to sing and does a cover of The Bangles' 'Eternal Flame', prompting Carrie to proclaim her performance "sensational".

Chris is up next with Van Morrison's 'Brown Eyed Girl' and he throws a few dance moves into the mix. Afterwards Kevin is full of praise, saying he has the dancing potential to be the next Justin Timberlake.

Then it's Katie's turn, and she gives it her all as she performs a somewhat nervous version of LeAnn Rimes' 'Can't Fight The Moonlight'. "Her tuning was quite a way under the note. It was quite difficult for Katie tonight," Carrie comments, to a chorus of boos.

In the meantime, the audience are treated to performances that are so good even Richard Park gets excited! Ainslie and Marli raise the temperature with their sexy rendition of Steve Harley's 'Make Me Smile (Come Up And See Me)', "Absolutely sensational. Exactly what we want to see coming out of the Academy" Richard declares.

Lemar captivates everyone when he belts out a flawless rendition of Al Green's 'Let's Stay Together', which had also been showcased on Steve Wright's Radio Two show the day before. Camilla and Nigel impress everyone with their duet of Luther Vandross's 'Ain't No Stopping Us Now', although Carrie deems Camilla to be "a little under the note" as well. David, Malachi and Sinead's version of Cyndi Lauper's 'Time After Time' goes down a treat and judging by the huge smile on David's face, he's having the time of his life.

who voted for who?

MALACHI ▶ KATIE
NIGEL ▶ CHRIS
MARLI ▶ KATIE
SINEAD ▶ KATIE
LEMAR ▶ CHRIS
CAMILLA ▶ KATIE
AINSLIE ▶ CHRIS
DAVID ▶ CHRIS
PIPPA ▶ KATIE

After a tense wait, Cat announces that Pippa has won over the public with a huge 48% of the votes. It's now up to the students to decide whether Katie or Chris should stay in the Academy. Taking their seats on stage, each student writes down the name of the probationer they want to save and stand in turn, to explain their decision.

As the students' votes are revealed it's neck and neck, and it comes down to Pippa to make the final decision. "This is the hardest thing I've ever had to do apart from being on probation," she says, before revealing that Katie has got her vote. Katie responds by crying, saying that she feels Chris should stay in. "I'm going to work so hard," she promises everyone through her sobs.

The final word goes to a disappointed Chris. "Be good, enjoy yourselves and God bless. I'll see you soon," he smiles at everyone, before heading off to catch up with his family and friends.

Ainslie and Marli get up close and personal back at the Academy and romp on Malachi's bed. "You're so sexy!" Ainslie tells her as she giggles joyfully. Sadly, their little party is broken up when Malachi wanders in to find out what all the noise is about. Who knows what might happen between the flirty pair in the future?

interview
Chris

WE CAUGHT UP WITH CHARMER CHRIS — THE SECOND STUDENT TO BE EXPELLED FROM FAME ACADEMY — TO FIND OUT ABOUT THAT KISS WITH MARLI AND HIS PLANS FOR THE FUTURE.

How do you feel about being expelled from Fame Academy?
Fine, because the whole thing has probably been the best experience of my life. I've met some incredibly talented individuals and loved sharing some special moments with them. I felt privileged to be a part of something that was aimed specifically at people with talent. I'm excited about what's going to happen and how things will progress from here.

How did you feel when the other students were voting to keep you or Katie in?
It was weird because it was down to Pippa's vote and I couldn't see what she'd written. I'd said to the guys all week not to worry, but when it came down to it no one could look at me, especially the girls.

Was there anyone you were surprised didn't vote for you?
I thought Sinead and Malachi might and I was a little bit surprised that they didn't. I mean, I may be wrong, but I think that they didn't necessarily vote on the performance on the night, but on how the rest of the weeks were going to pan out as a result. There was a bit of tactical voting going on. But fair play to them. I might have done the same thing.

Were you pleased with your probation performance?
Yes, absolutely over the moon. Everything seemed to go my way. Apart from the vote, obviously!

Do you think you deserved to go?
No. I don't think the teachers or the students or the public really got the chance to know me well enough.

Richard said he thought you did deserve to go...
Well, I don't think they gave me enough chance to show what I can do. There's so much left in me and it's just a shame the teachers judged me on my personality when my effort was one hundred and fifty percent.

The teachers also said they didn't think you were always yourself in the Academy. Do you agree?
I think everyone, including myself, found it hard to be one hundred percent themselves in that environment. It has a unique and twisted weirdness about it. I'm the sort of person who will guard myself, but I think I was myself more than it came across.

Best and worst experiences in the Academy?
The worst was probably just getting up every morning and having Richard shouting at the top of his voice. I also felt incredibly exposed with all the cameras there. The best moment was in one of our songwriting lessons when Lemar came up with a song idea about Pippa, Katie

and I being on probation. That was so incredibly touching. I know Lemar is going to be a huge star, and it was amazing that someone so modest with so much talent had written something for us.

Who did you become close to?
Ainslie. We kicked off on the wrong foot, but then he realised that I was just like him; a little bit scared and a little bit vulnerable, and I disguise it by appearing overconfident. But I genuinely got along with everyone.

You snogged Marli in the Truth or Dare game, but did you actually fancy any of the girls?
No. I don't think the kiss was a big deal. It was just a bit of fun. I wasn't in the show for love, I was there to find out a little bit more about myself.

What was the biggest lesson Fame Academy taught you?
To stay true to yourself and not to try and be anyone that you're not. It's about continuing to believe in yourself no matter what criticism is thrown at you. You've got to remember who you are, where you've come from, who your friends are and how lucky you are to have this gift.

What was the worst criticism you got?
Probably that I force my ego upon other people. I though that was quite harsh and it hurt a bit.

What did you miss while you were in there?
My phone, a few of my mates, my family and not being able to pick up a paper or magazine or my guitar. I didn't miss alcohol that much, even though it probably seemed like I did!

Who do you think has the best chance of winning?
Ainslie and Lemar because they are great characters and they're quite unique.

Who do you think will be next out?
Katie, just based on performance. I think she would come across much better if she had stuck to her classical style.

Would you have suited the pop star lifestyle?
I wouldn't have complained about it! But part of me would have found it difficult to accept the prize because I want to work hard and feel like I've earned the right to have that kind of lifestyle. But at the same time I think I would have secretly loved it.

You were in a pop band for three years, weren't you?
Yes, we were a five-piece boy/girl band called Red Alert. We used to tour the country and support bands like Atomic Kitten and Five. We came close to a couple of record deals, but it wasn't to be.

You've said you'd like to try acting. What would you like to do?
I'd like to get my teeth into something dark and serious like 'The Matrix'; something sci-fi and a bit different. I really would love to try my hand at acting at some point.

What's next for you?
I've always been a singer songwriter and that's my passion, so I'm going to carry on. I've never aspired to be popular or famous, but of course the more success you have, the more famous you become. I'm just going to keep taking steps in the right direction and hope for the best.

Fame Academy Style

WE CAUGHT UP WITH THE FAME ACADEMY STYLIST EXTRAORDINAIRE KIRSTY DRURY, IN THE SECOND TO LAST WEEK OF THE SHOW TO FIND OUT ALL THE STUDENTS' STYLE SECRETS.

Camilla

Camilla really liked bright colours, especially pink. She had a great figure and was very comfortable with how she looked, so she liked short skirts and lots of denim, quite figure-hugging stuff.

She's really into J-Lo, Aaliyah and Kylie's looks. She had a really clear idea of what she liked and didn't like and said from the word go that she'd like to be a kind of black Britney.

She was quite sexy to dress and into trend-leading clothes. She didn't want to follow fashion too much and she liked being quite directional.

Chris

I didn't have much time to develop Chris's style because he was expelled in the second week, but he was an interesting mixture of street and smart. He can go both ways.

He's so good looking that he suited absolutely everything and he's got beautiful skin as well. His influences are Frank Sinatra, Lenny Kravitz and Justin Timberlake and he said his ideal look is a classic 50's gangster with a sharp made to measure suit. He's was also quite into the 70's retro feel, but didn't like very baggy, oversized clothing at all.

Katie

Katie didn't really know what she wanted. She knew what she didn't like, but she wouldn't say it to me. She would say it back to someone else and forget she was on camera 24 hours a day!

She's got an amazing figure and everything looks good on her. She likes the style of Jennifer Anniston, Victoria Beckham and Kylie, but when I started working with her I kept her quite young and girlie as she was the baby of the group. But as time went on she grew up a lot and I felt that her clothing could start to grow up with her and get a bit sexier. Her look was quite Britney in that she would wear cropped trousers and have her tummy out. But after a couple of weeks I tried to make her more of a London girl, so she wore the Pucci dress. That was the one she absolutely hated wearing. I think it was a bit scary for her!

Ainslie

Ainslie is an absolute dream to dress, he's one of my favourites. When we first talked about his style he said that he was quite up for going out a limb and doing something a bit different. He's not into label clothing and he had his retro jeans, slogan t-shirts, vintage thing going on, so I tried to introduce a new look for him as I think that's a bit dated.

He's up for being quite androgynous and doesn't mind if he looks quite girlie and I love that about him. He's got such a sense of style. He likes anything that's quite skinny fit and doesn't mind showing off his tummy.

His main influences are David Bowie, Jimmy Paige and The Strokes and I often dress him in women's clothing. On last week's show he was wearing a Zara suit,

this week he's going to be in some Karen Millen trousers, and he's also worn Top Shop. He looks great in women's clothes. They fit him brilliantly.

Lemar

Lemar wants to be street but smart, sophisticated and stand apart from the crowd. I like to have both of those influences in his outfits. He's got a great sense of style and looks good in everything. When I'm styling him I think along the lines of David Beckham.

We've had a variety of styles for him for the show and he's up for trying anything. I never wanted him to look too street and typical black singer in an oversized top, trousers, cap and jewels, because direction-wise with him we can be a bit more outrageous because he can carry anything off.

Stylistically, he really likes Al Green and R Kelly and he'd like to be seen as a style setter. He's got a fantastic body and he's not afraid to show it off, but he hates his feet!

Malachi

When I first met Malachi he'd flown over having just done communion in Ireland and he looked so square in his smart shirt and sensible trousers and really short hair. He was the one I was most concerned about. I was thinking: "What am I going to do with this guy?!" But he's the one who blossomed the most in some ways.

Once we started discovering things that suited him – like for instance boot cut

34

jeans because he's really tall – the change was amazing. The leather jackets came next and he started to look pretty sexy and then when we got him into a suit, it was like "Wow!" He really does suit a suit.

Malachi loves jewellery, and funnily enough his main style influence is Graham Norton. He told me he wanted to look like him the first time I met him, which is quite surprising. He also liked Bono from U2.

Marli

Marli was wonderful. She's got a really unique style already and has a beautiful face. She's got a lovely little figure and she was really easy to dress. But I didn't feel like we got enough time to experiment as much as I would have liked to.

She was really into the Ava Gardener look - she really liked that kind of glam era – but she mixed it up with a bit of Madonna. She's quite chameleon-like and can wear many different looks and still make them look like her own. She looks fantastic in hats and was always up for trying something new.

Marli has got great arms, shoulders and cleavage, so we showed them off a lot. She loved emerald and jade colours, corsets and hairpieces and vintage one-offs. But wasn't into baggy clothes like combat trousers, and she didn't like earrings. In fact, she didn't wear much jewellery at all; she was more into making a statement with the outfit than with accessories.

Nigel

He won't like me saying this, but Nigel was kind of stuck in 1992/93. He was a proper club man in the mad shirts and the tight trousers but he was open to trying new things.

His influences were Lenny Kravitz and Michael Hutchence. He said he wanted to be different, but that he didn't have much opportunity in Doncaster!

Nigel was very conscious of his physique in that he didn't think he was thin enough, so we'd try and get nice fitted things for him. He looked good in boot cut trousers because, in his own words, he's got bowlegs. He also got quite big feet so if you put him in narrow or tapered trousers he'd end up with these huge boats! He really loved his jewellery – anything a bit ethnic – and he was quite Bryan Adams in that he like his jeans to be a bit roughed up.

Pippa

Pippa was great. She was a proper Northern club girl and loved anything glitzy and glamorous with jewellery. She loved pink and glitter and sparkle. I loved her style. It was slightly tacky and quite Spice Girls, but I thought she looked great. She had an amazingly flat stomach so she looked great in cropped tops, too.

Her influences were Madonna, early days of Britney and Kylie. She likes to stand apart from the crowd and be quite individual and raunchy. She was also up for trying new looks.

In the second to last week she was in the Academy I put her in a waistcoat and jeans tucked into boots. She didn't like it at first, but then she wore it and loved it. I think if she'd stayed longer she would have become a real London girl and been quite directional with her look.

Ashley

Ashley was quite retro and jazz funk. He was into 70's looks and liked wooden jewellery, brown leather and funnel neck knits and he really liked hats. He definitely

didn't like the tight t-shirt, lots of flesh or the Will Young look. His influences were more Jay Kay, Groove Armada and Jamie Oliver. He wasn't keen on showing off his body as he was quite hairy. I didn't get too much of a style going on for him because he was out so quickly, but I would have gone for that vintage, 70's, Lenny Kravitz style had he stayed on.

Sinead

Sinead doesn't like to follow trends. She likes vintage clothing, one off items and customising clothes. Her style is quite Gwen Stefani, but not as hard. She likes to be a bit more bohemian, but all the flowy gypsy stuff that's around at the moment doesn't suit her that much.

She looks good in anything that's got a nipped in waist and she looks great in trousers and high heels.

She's got such a beautiful face, absolutely amazing, plus she really suits black clothes. She loves bright colours so we usually use bright accessories like hats, which look fantastic on her.

David

David didn't really know much about his direction at first. He has a very casual look and can sometimes look a bit boy band, which we're trying to avoid. I wanted to give him a style that has maturity about it so he's not in that boy band mould. I want him to look sexy rather than boyish. He loves big baggy trousers and trainers, but we try not to do that too much for shows as we want to make him look a bit slicker.

His influences are David Beckham, Jamie Theakston and he really likes the Rat Pack look. He's kind of up for anything and loves leather jackets and jewellery, but he doesn't like sleeveless tops.

POOR NAOMI HAD TO LEAVE THE ACADEMY DUE TO THROAT PROBLEMS. BUT SHE MANAGED TO FIND HER VOICE AND HAVE A GOSSIP ABOUT HER FELLOW STUDENTS.

Are you really disappointed about having to leave Fame Academy?
Of course I am a bit, but it's been the best experience and I've learnt so much about the industry. I would never have experienced all of those things if I hadn't been in Fame Academy. I've got no regrets. I'm an eternal optimist and this is just a minor setback.

You shed a few tears when you left. How hard was it saying goodbye to everyone?
It was so hard. They were such a nice group of people and they were so lovely to me when I was leaving. I think it was good because I found out at seven o'clock on Sunday night I was leaving, and then left at nine on Monday morning, so I didn't have much time to pine or worry about it.

What do you think would have happened if you had stayed in the Academy?
I think if my voice had been on full form I would have been alright. I'm a hard worker so I would have been fine in Kevin's classes, and I would love to have got more of a chance to experience Pam's songwriting classes. But the other guys are so talented that you just don't know. I'd like to think that I could have stayed in for a few more weeks.

What were your best and worst experiences?
The best were just being with everybody and having a laugh. The worst moment was after I'd seen the specialist because I was devastated when I found out I had to leave. It was also awful when Richard told me I couldn't do one of the singing classes, and I had to sit outside and listen to everyone. I so wanted to be in there with them.

Who are you going to miss most?
I think I'll miss Ainsley and Malachi most. I'll miss all the girls, but on a one to one level Ainslie and Malachi were my closest mates.

You were initially worried about getting on with the girls in the house. Why was that?
I usually get on better with guys, but actually I ended up getting on with the girls and it was nice sharing the room with them. They were really good people.

Do you think you'll stay in touch with everyone?
I hope so. I've already been in touch with Ashley, and hopefully we'll all meet up when they get out. It's nice that it's just one person a week coming out so you get time to see them.

How did you feel about being watched constantly in the Academy?

I didn't really think about it while I was in there, but whenever I see videos of us in the Academy, it's a real reality shock. But really it's just like an exaggeration of me being at drama school.

Are you going back to drama school?

No. I still had two years of my degree left, but now I want to work really hard and concentrate on the music business. That's where my dream is so I'm going to keep going with it. Hopefully once my throat is better I'll come back stronger and better than ever. That's my plan!

How do you feel about David replacing you?

I knew him really well from the Glasgow and London auditions, so I don't think there could have been a better person to take my place. I feel no bitterness or resentment towards him, I'm just really pleased for him.

All of you girls fancied Jeremy, didn't you?

Yes, he's a really good guy. Marli especially fancies him. And Katie is having real, real fantasies about Kevin. She's loving him.

Jeremy appears to flirt with the girls a lot...

Oh yes! He has a very small personal space. I can't wait to see him at the aftershow party when he's not having to look after us all and he can have a drink and relax. I think he'll really go for it. I would love to see him snog Marli. I would love it. It would be so amusing!

Ashley has said that he thinks you and Ainslie were going to get it together. Do you think you would have done if you'd stayed in?

Ainslie's a very good boy and is in love with his girlfriend, so I don't think anything like that would have happened. We just became good mates.

Ashley also said he thinks Lemar and Camilla might get it together...

Lemar has a girlfriend of six years, but he definitely likes Camilla, and Camilla definitely likes him. But I don't think Lemar would be foolish enough to do anything live on television. I think there's a real chemistry between them so I'd like to see something happen when they get out.

Are there any other romances blossoming in there?

I think Sinead and Malachi make a beautiful couple, but I think Malachi is a wee bit too much of a charmer and just enjoys flirting.

Who do you think will be next out of the Academy?

This Friday it's Katie, Chris and Pippa, and I think if Chris doesn't get the public vote, he'll be voted out by the students. And I think if it's between Katie and Pippa, Pippa will get voted to stay in by the students.

Who do you think is going to win?

I would like to see Ainslie win, I think he deserves to. But I think Lemar or Marli may win. But then I can also see David or Sinead winning. And you never know, Nigel might do well as he got the public vote. I can't wait to see what's going to happen.

AINSLIE

HE'S OF A
CONSISTENTLY HIGH
STANDARD AS
A SONGWRITER.
I LOVE HIS STYLE
PAM

I LOVE HIM,
ABSOLUTELY LOVE
HIM, GREAT VOICE,
GREAT LOOKING,
NAUGHTY BUT NICE
CARRIE

GRADE A

Saturday

The students are impressed with the previous night's performance, as are the teachers. Carrie's favourites are Ainslie and Marli, while Richard tells Nigel: "you were like a legendary soul singer with a dozen chart hits," and that it was: "the best show we have done so far."

Carrie teaches the group some relaxation techniques during their afternoon vocal class and is blown away by David's performance of his own material in their one-to-one session. Pam likes Malachi's songwriting style but tells him that he needs to start thinking in more commercial terms. Jeremy's new game is pairing the students off to act out song lyrics. The students are in fits of laughter as Pippa dresses up like a man, Nigel dons a bra, and Malachi stuffs socks down his pants. Ainslie has a deep and meaningful with David and admits: "Before I even met you I disliked you. I felt like I had my own identity and then another cute Scottish bloke turned up."

Sunday

Kevin has the students begging for mercy as he puts them through their paces in a particularly tough dance class, then meets with Richard to discuss the students. He feels that Camilla and Katie need to raise their game whilst Nigel has made fantastic improvements.

Carrie gets Malachi to sing whilst kneeling in an attempt to stop him thinking about his body so much when he performs.

Pam announces to the group that they are to be split into three groups so they can write lyrics for a backing track, which has been provided by a famous mystery songwriter. There is talk of the track being released as a single if it's good enough. The groups are:

▸ Nigel, Lemar and Camilla
▸ Malachi, Sinead, David and Katie
▸ Marli, Ainslie and Pippa

Monday

It's Grade Day and concerns are expressed for Sinead's throat problems, as well as Marli's "personal problems". It's announced that Katie, Camilla and David will be Singing for Survival on Friday's live showdown. David laughs and says: "I don't believe it. Bring it on!" Katie looks disappointed, while Camilla sheds a few tears.

A surprised Ainslie is named Grade A student and is told that as a reward he will be attending the Q awards that night with the student of his choice – Malachi!

The students continue to add lyrics to the mystery backing track. Pam cites Lemar's group's effort as the best and announces that the students will be writing lyrics around their melody, much to the disappointment of Ainslie who is desperate to be top scribe.

Ainslie decides that a slick of eyeliner is in order to get that authentic 'rock god' look for his night out. On their return, Malachi and Ainslie are greeted by Katie, who tells them that Jeremy has taken all the other students to a private club. Malachi soon discovers the jokers hiding in cupboards and behind curtains.

Tuesday

Ainslie and Malachi are feeling the effects of their rock star night out. Malachi struggles though Kevin's dance class, and is forced to do extra sit-ups after Kevin accuses him of slacking.

Carrie announces to the amazed students that diva Shania Twain will be taking a Masterclass the next day. The students who have been chosen to join her are Pippa, Sinead, Lemar and Nigel. The foursome have to prepare by learning the words to Shania's smash hit 'You're Still The One'.

Camilla has a vocal class with Carrie, and admits she is feeling really upset about being put on probation. Carrie offers some comforting words.

Nigel, Lemar and Malachi rehearse the Tom Jones classic 'Sex Bomb' with Carrie and Jo.

Malachi loves every moment of playing out his loverman role but there are more tears from Katie during her song for survival vocal class with Carrie. She admits that she's terrified of messing up again and the pressure is really getting to her. Best pals Ainslie and Malachi have a chat about the fact Malachi has made neither A Grade or probation yet. Ainslie tells Malachi he is: "An appalling dancer!" Ainslie and Malachi land in trouble when Jeremy catches them messing around, playing music and shouting in the dance studio, having indulged in a glass of wine...

Wednesday

The Headmaster and Kevin meet up for a chat about the probationers' progress. Kevin says that David has a positive mental attitude, Camilla hasn't realised her full potential, while Katie is still thinking of her time in the Academy as a holiday.

Kevin is amazed by Pippa, Lemar and Nigel's performances in his dance class, getting them to show off their talents for the rest of the students, but there are tears aplenty when Ainslie and Pippa open their mail. Ainslie gets emotional over a letter from his family and Pippa has to be comforted when she gets an unimpressively short letter from her boyfriend.

The three probationers gather in the kitchen to discuss the upcoming Showdown. David says that whoever goes out has to promise to get completely drunk. When Katie leaves, a worried Camilla and David carry on chatting about how good Katie is sounding. Superstar Shania Twain arrives at the Academy and is greeted by the excited students. Shania tells Ainslie that she has already heard 'Keep Me a Secret' – the track he's written with Sinead and Malachi – and loves it. Nigel admits that Shania's super-ballad 'You're Still The One' was the first song at his wedding. After a Q&A session and a lot of nervous singing from the students, Shania admits that she's impressed

by the students, especially when Sinead, Malachi and Ainslie do a special performance of 'Keep Me a Secret' for the ecstatic star. However, the glory of 'Keep Me a Secret' weighs heavy on Ainslie's heart and he apologises to Sinead over dinner for appearing to take all the credit for it.

Thursday

The teachers gather to discuss how Shania's Masterclass went and all agree it was a roaring success. "She was so down to earth. They were so nervous, but she really put their minds at ease," says Carrie. The tutor then reveals that in her opinion, Katie will be leaving the Academy next, while Kevin refuses to reveal who he thinks will be for the chop: "Every time I make a guess I'm wrong".

The students practise for Friday's Showdown. Kevin suggests Ainslie and Lemar take inspiration from the facial expressions Shania makes when she sings, but Ainslie admits in an intimate chat with Malachi that he hasn't really enjoyed his Grade A status. The students sit down in the lounge with Richard, listening to his showbiz tales. Sinead misses the gossip because she's busy having her golden locks dyed red in the girls' bedroom. When the probationers deliver their speeches to the other students in the lounge, Katie tells them: "I have had the best experience of my life and learned so much. You must all do what you think is best."

David has everyone in fits when he says: "Let me start by telling you a story about a boy who appeared on a well known BBC TV show, failed to get in properly, but managed to get in by the grace of God. Now it was very short lived, and he had to go after only a week and a bit. And that's a sick ending kids. It's up to you lot to give it a happy ending!"

Camilla's speech, on the other hand, is short and tearful: "It's been great, but it's down to you guys," she tells them in between sobs.

KATIE **SHE PUT IN A DISAPPOINTING PERFORMANCE LAST WEEK**
RICHARD

DAVID **FOR ME HE'S BOY BAND MATERIAL. I JUST DON'T SEE HIM AS A SOLO ARTIST**
CARRIE

CAMILLA **DRIVING ALL HER SKILLS TOGETHER AND MAKING A BIG IMPRESSION IS SOMETHING SHE'S FOUND HARD TO DO**
RICHARD

ON PROBATION

Sing for Survival

THE STUDENTS MAKE THEIR WAY DOWN TO SHEPPERTON STUDIOS TO PREPARE FOR TONIGHT'S LIVE SHOW. DAVID IS FEELING SURPRISINGLY CALM, DESPITE HAVING TO SING FOR SURVIVAL IN JUST A FEW HOURS. BUT IT'S A DIFFERENT STORY FOR KATIE AND CAMILLA WHO JUST CAN'T CONTROL THEIR NERVES.

We caught up with world famous songstress Shania Twain for a chat about – what else? – Fame Academy!

Why did you decide to get involved with Fame Academy?
I think it's fascinating. If I had had the opportunity to do something like that when I was younger, I would totally have done it.

You didn't go to stage school or anything, did you?
No, I got my experience in clubs. But I dreamt about it when I was younger and thought how much I would have loved the opportunity to go to performing arts school or something, but it was too expensive. At one time people thought music wasn't a real career and couldn't take it seriously, but now I think there are ways to discover if you are talented and things can be nurtured. I think it's a cool concept.

Have you got a favourite Fame Academy student?
I can't pick favourites! I like the way different people do different things. I think they all have so much potential. I'm very excited to see how they're all going to do.

The show is soon to begin and things are manic. Katie's boyfriend is late as he's been caught up in a car crash, but thankfully he gets there in the nick of time and joins the other excited family members. The students and teachers take their places, with Camilla, Katie and

David standing on the stage awaiting their fate. Camilla calms noticeably when she catches sight of her parents and waves maniacally to them. The other students also take the opportunity to smile and wave to their friends and family and Sinead is keen to show off her new hairdo to a pal sitting across the studio.

Cat and Patrick stride up the walkway signalling the start of the show and the crowd go mad. Camilla is first to Sing For Survival and slinks her way through 'Genie In a Bottle'. Afterwards Carrie has a few criticisms to make: "I think she had a few pitching problems," she says, as the crowd boo. David goes next and adds some very "David" touches to Ronan Keating's 'When You Say Nothing At All'. Once again, Carrie is critical, stating: "I just don't think he's got it," to yet more boos. The final probationer to take to the stage is Katie. She gets to sing her favourite song, 'Over The Rainbow', as Malachi, Lemar, Pippa and Marli clasp their hands in a praying position and appear to be willing her on. Their prayers obviously work and Carrie is full of praise for her performance.

Next it's up to Shania Twain to pick a favourite, but she plumps for a diplomatic: "I thought they were all good." Fair point, Mrs.Twain. Malachi, Nigel and Lemar perform their rendition of 'Sex Bomb' to massive cheers from the ladies. There's praise indeed for Nigel who Shania says has: "that Tom Jones rasp."

It's the girls' turn next and Pippa, Marli and Sinead belt out Shola Ama's 'You Might Need Somebody'. Then it's time for the first student-penned song to be performed outside of the Academy walls. Ainslie, Sinead and Malachi belt out 'Keep Me a Secret', which goes down amazingly well, and the three students look delighted at the reaction of the roaring crowd.

The results of the public vote are in and Katie, Camilla and David stand on the stage waiting for Cat to read out the verdict. David is stunned to hear that the public has decided to save him and he has 50% of the overall votes.

Now it's up to the students to decide if Camilla or Katie will stay. It seems to take forever for the students to write their choices down, especially Ainslie who looks completely traumatised by the whole affair. But a choice must be made and when the votes have been counted up it's revealed that this week Camilla will be leaving the Academy. Katie cries, Ainslie throws his pen on the floor and Camilla takes her defeat gracefully as her fellow students give her a goodbye hug. Hey, that's showbiz.

The show was rounded off this week by the Academy star guest, Shania Twain, who belted out her new hit single 'I'm Gonna Get You Good'. Needless to say the teachers didn't have too many complaints about her amazing performance!

who voted for who?

SINEAD ▸ KATIE
NIGEL ▸ CAMILLA
PIPPA ▸ KATIE
AINSLIE ▸ KATIE
MARLI ▸ CAMILLA
MALACHI ▸ KATIE
LEMAR ▸ CAMILLA
DAVID ▸ KATIE

WEEK THREE

Interview
Camilla

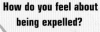

How do you feel about being expelled?

Disappointed with my fellow students. I think I deserved to stay and there's a lot more in me that the public didn't get to see. But I'm not bitter or resentful, it's a game at the end of the day. Although I do get a bit jealous when I watch the show live.

And you're also the first girl to be expelled...

Yes, I don't like that title at all. But I'm okay.

Are you shocked you were expelled?

Yes, and I'm surprised at the amount of people who I've met since I've been out who are shocked! When I was on stage listening to what the teachers were saying about me I thought: "Wow, I must have been really rubbish." But when I came off stage everyone was saying I was really good. Then after I'd seen my performance I really didn't think I should have gone. It makes me feel a

bit angry with my fellow students and also with the teachers. Pam was actually crying during the Live Showdown because the audience booed her when she criticised me. Kevin had to console her.

Which students are you most angry with?

Sinead, Ainslie and Malachi particularly because they're all songwriters, and I thought they'd all value that in me and see my potential. Katie doesn't write songs and she wasn't really getting that into the lessons. She was viewing the Academy as a little holiday away from home, but I felt like I had so much to give. I think there was a bit of tactical voting going on, to be honest.

Were you nervous when all the students were voting?

Kind of. I have to admit I was shocked when the public voted for David as I thought it would be Katie who got the vote. Then I immediately thought the students' vote would be really hard because it was between me and Katie. I tried to detach myself emotionally, although I was really happy when Marli and Lemar voted for me because they were the ones I cared about most. I would have been really torn up if they hadn't.

Now you've left, what do you feel most disappointed about?

I'm really gutted that I didn't get to do the Masterclass with Lionel Ritchie. I would have

loved to have done that. I'm really annoyed with Pam Sheyne as well as she said I was a natural songwriter, but she put me on probation.

You've watched some of the shows since you've been out. Are you shocked by anything you've seen?

Yes, when Ainslie, Marli and David were bitching about Pam picking my group's melody for the Lionel Ritchie track. I was quite surprised about that. I've also seen Malachi trying to be a real ladies man. I saw his willy dangling out of his underwear and I think it might have been caught on camera once as well.

Who do you think is playing up to the cameras in the Academy?

Ainslie knows how to play the game, he plays up to the cameras very well. He says he doesn't want to win it and that it's everyone else's competition, but he so wants to win it. But I do think he's really good, he's got star quality. I didn't realise just how much he's playing the game until I got out and saw him. He was very distant to me in the few days leading up to the Live Showdown and was suddenly much closer to Katie, which is weird because before he didn't have any time for her. I found his behaviour a bit odd.

Would you have pulled out all the stops to win if you'd stayed in?

Oh yes, I'd have tried everything. I'd have had an affair with Lemar! No, I'm only joking.

Ah, but are you? Was there any romance between the two of you?

No, I really like him, but we're professional and he's got a girlfriend so I wouldn't even go there. He was very supportive and he was always someone I could talk to. And I think vice versa.

Who do you think will win?

I think Lemar has a good chance because he's very popular. But then, Ainslie is very popular too. I think it's close between those two. As long as people don't boot Lemar out at the first opportunity because they see him as a threat. Sinead is very talented too, and she wants it badly. I also think Marli has a good chance and I think David is coming up. He is proving to be very competitive and very hungry for it.

What are you going to do next?

I want to get in the studio and get writing and get some good material together. I'd like to release something quite soon. The sound I love is the Neptunes, R'n'B, Nelly and Kelly Rowland style sound, but with commercial elements. I love writing songs, and that's the kind of angle I'd love to go for.

Who do you think will be next out?

Out of Katie, Nigel and Pippa who are on probation, I think Nigel will get the public vote and it will be between the girls for the student vote. That would be funny because then Pippa would know how I felt, because she didn't vote for me! She voted for Katie instead.

Who do you think you'll stay close to when it's all over?

Lemar. He's a sweet guy and I hope it doesn't get to much for him in there. It's quite intense and we were a good release for each other. We knew we could rely on each other, and I don't think there's anyone else like that in there for him. He doesn't really bond with the other guys as they're all a bit silly. He's quite serious, and they're all whipping each other's butts and stuff. And with the girls, Pippa and Katie are a bit silly, and I would say Marli is the only one he could talk to.

How did you get on with the teachers?

I got on fine with them. It's only when I got out that I realised that some of them were a bit horrible about me. I couldn't believe that Kevin said I was two weeks behind on the dancing when Malachi or Katie couldn't get a single dance step right. And he put me on probation. But while I was in there I got on well with all of them and really respected them. Carrie taught me a lot and I'm definitely going to miss the vocal technique lessons.

Which were you favourite lessons?

I really enjoyed the songwriting and singing lessons, they were great. I loved the dance lessons, although I hated the stretching so much. I loved the dancing, I'm just not very confident. I've got a lot of natural rhythm and when I get a dance routine in my head I can bring a lot of flava to it, but I don't get the routines as quickly as people like Marli.

What are the main things Fame Academy taught you?

"To compete always!" as Richard Park would say. Seriously though, it taught me discipline and I was getting a lot better at picking up the dance routines. It taught me some good singing techniques, although I think I need to continue with that. It taught me to be more competitive because I think I was a bit too laid back in there and not as competitive as I should have been. I thought everyone was being laid back, but now I realise that most people were actually being very competitive. It taught me to appreciate my life and my freedom and it taught me to have a lot of self-belief because I got criticised a lot, and that showed me that you've got to believe in yourself even when other people don't.

How did you find living with everyone so closely?

It was hard, but I learnt to live with other people with a lot of patience. Usually I'm quite hot tempered and I can blow up about things, but in there I was very calm and I let things brush over me. I had to.

Did you want to blow up at anyone in particular?

Not really, people were generally cool to get on with. Pippa irritated me a bit because she was quite moany and self-obsessed and kept saying she was a princess. And Marli sometimes worries about things and gets into things too deeply and she needs to get on with things. But all in all, people were great.

Who do you think is feeling the pressure in the Academy?

Katie, and also Pippa because after she got the public vote she felt like a bit of a star, and started giving me advice and stuff. So I think the shock of being on probation has bought her back down to earth.

Would you do it all again?

Definitely. I had a great time. You're getting exquisite teaching, you're doing a lot of performing, and it taught me all about live TV. It was an absolutely amazing experience.

Saturday

Ainslie goes for an early morning stroll in the grounds and has a long chat with himself, as well as a bit of a rant about Fame Academy. Is the pressure of being Grade A student getting to him?

When the group watch a video of their performances from the previous night Carrie praises Katie and Ainslie for their performances, but admits she wasn't overly impressed with Marli, David or Lemar's efforts. Poor Marli sheds a few tears on Carrie's shoulder and admits that she's devastated about her performance at the Live Showdown. Pippa, Ainslie and Katie do their best to cheer her up, with Katie telling her: "You're so amazing." Sinead and Malachi have a play flirt, sorry, fight, during which Malachi draws a moustache on Sinead.

There's laughs a-plenty as the boys gather in the lounge armed with a red wig and do some spectacular impressions of Carrie, followed by a pre-dinner sing-in in the lounge with Richard and Pam in attendance. A perkier Marli performs her own song, 'Come Closer', which impresses everyone and Pippa gains much praise when she performs her self-penned number, 'No One Knows'.

Sunday

Jeremy and Richard both agree that Marli has had too much of a fuss made of her, while Jeremy feels Ainslie may be getting a tad big for his boots. He also reveals that Malachi is expecting to be out on probation this week, Katie is on borrowed time and Nigel has stopped winding everyone up quite so much.

David reveals hidden depths during a vocal lesson when he showcases his piano playing abilities and performs some of his own material to a stunned Carrie and Jo. "This changes everything. To find a good-looking person who can sing is so difficult. To find a good-looking writer-musician, you go from being average to being the full package," Carrie tells the happy lad, whom she'd only recently labelled 'boy band material'.

Richard announces that soul legend Lionel Ritchie will be taking the next Masterclass. The students will be split into two groups to work on the backing track which has been provided by Lionel himself. There's exciting news inside the Academy when Carrie interrupts dinner to crack open the champagne and announce that Katie's sister has given birth, making her the proud auntie of a baby girl. "That's amazing!" enthuses Katie.

Later, in preparation for Halloween, the students stay up late telling far-fetched ghost stories and scare the living daylights out of each other.

Monday

The teachers have their weekly meeting to discuss the students' progress. Comments include how Marli's confidence has been knocked, Nigel needs to be less cabaret and Ainslie is struggling a bit, while Malachi has been lucky to escape expulsion so far.

As for Sinead? Kevin, Carrie and Pam agree she's doing brilliantly and despite Richard's initial reticence, she is named Grade A student. There are cheers all round and huge smiles from Sinead: her reward is not only to have her hair dyed back to its natural blonde by a top stylist, but she will be attending the premiere and party of 'Our House – The Madness Musical' in London's West End, and chooses Pippa to accompany her. There are few smiles from the probationers – Pippa, Katie and Nigel – when their names are announced.

Malachi and Ainslie have fun in the grounds pretending to be, er, farmers. Pippa and Sinead spend ages getting glammed up for their big night and while they head off to live it up, the rest of the students lie on the floor humming and gargling as top speech and language therapist Annabel Bosenquet teaches them breathing techniques. Later that night the students' bizarre behaviour includes Ainslie tweaking his nipples for ages, Malachi writing 'I love David' on Katie's leg, Katie giving Ainslie a manicure, and Malachi and Ainslie giving Katie a makeover.

Things get even weirder when Ainslie decides to spread grapes across the tablecloth in the dining room and suck them up one by one, before announcing: "I've gotta get out of here. I want out from under these lights. I'm sick of the sound of other people's f*****g music. I'm sick of the sound of other people singing and playing the piano." Thankfully a chat with Jeremy soon puts a smile back on his face.

Tuesday

Nigel is barely up for five minutes when he returns to bed with a migraine. Sinead is also in pain when she falls off the running machine and bumps her bum. It seems that her hangover has well and truly caught up with her. Thankfully, Pippa's not suffering as much as her partying pal and impresses Carrie with her rendition of Anastacia's 'I'm Outta Love' during her vocal class.

Malachi is feeling cheery after a phone call with his dad. The Irish fella had been worrying about what his family would think about his behaviour in the Academy – in particular the lads' rather odd practice of whipping each other's backsides – but his dad assures him he's "pleased as punch" with the way he's presenting himself.

The students are treated to an early Halloween party in the dance studio. "Please help yourself to the vampire blood complete with eyeballs!" Jeremy tells the students as they let out a cheer. Jeremy then tells the assembled students some spooky stories about the Fame Academy mansion, before leading them in a game of dares. David licks the inside of Nigel's ear, Marli performs a striptease much to the delight of the boys and

the distaste of Sinead, Sinead sucks Ainslie's belly button, while David plays the piano naked! "It was cool seeing a little naked guy playing the piano!" laughs Ainslie afterwards.

Wednesday

The students are woken at 6.45am by Kevin banging pans together over the loudspeaker. They are then forced to do a tough workout in the grounds as punishment for some of the students not wearing their microphones. Tsk.

Malachi is in trouble when Kevin catches him smoking, despite his assurances that he'd given

"I'VE GOTTA GET OUT OF HERE. I WANT OUT FROM UNDER THESE LIGHTS. I'M SICK OF THE SOUND OF OTHER PEOPLE'S F*****G MUSIC" AINSLIE

up. Richard welcomes legendary soul singer Lionel Ritchie to the Academy and gives him a brief rundown of the students' schedule. "Oh my God, those poor people. They're under pressure, man!" Lionel exclaims. The superstar even proves he's been keeping a close eye on them when he asks Sinead how her head is after her partying on Monday night!

The students join Lionel in the music room to perform their songs for him. First up are Ainslie, Marli, Pippa and Malachi, who showcase 'Now Is The Time', before Lemar, Katie, David, Nigel and Sinead belt out 'You Want Me To Want You'. "You have some great moments there," an impressed Lionel tells them, before giving them some valuable songwriting tips. When it comes to choosing a favourite, Lionel chooses 'You Want Me To Want You'. Pam takes the bull by the horns and asks the soul sensation: "How would you and Paul (Lionel's co-writer) feel about working on that particular track?" "I would like to!" is Lionel's answer, as the students look on wide-eyed. Lionel rounds off his day at Fame Academy by practising his duet with Lemar for Friday's Live Showdown. The pair will perform The Commodores' classic 'Easy', which Lionel wrote himself.

Thursday

It's Halloween and the spooky day has definitely affected Kevin: he initiates a big hug-in during his class. With the Live Showdown just a day

away, Nigel, Pippa and Katie do some cracking performances of their Songs For Survival for Kevin and Carrie. David, Malachi and Ainslie spend some time playing 'hide from the cameras' in the lounge. But it isn't all fun and games when Malachi gets yet another telling off from Kevin for smoking. "You keep lying to me. I don't like liars. I don't care that you smoke. I asked you if you smoked and you said to me, 'Yeah, I have given up' and then I see you outside smoking. Why lie to me?" Kevin asks the worried looking Irishman.

The students spend the afternoon rehearsing at Shepperton Studios and then it's time for Katie, Pippa and Nigel to pack their bags in case they leave the Academy the following night. Pippa and Katie are distracted when a parcel full of cosmetics arrives for them, as well as some clothes for Marli and Pippa after some of theirs were ruined in the laundry. It's David who is most excited about their booty and promptly applies a face pack.

Nigel takes the opportunity to make an early goodbye speech just in case he is expelled, and heaps praise upon his fellow students telling Lemar he is "amazingly talented", Marli that she is "genuinely honest", and describes Ainslie as "Mr Originality". He also admits to Katie that he wrote the one and only fan letter she received that morning as she'd seemed a bit down the day before. Richard tells the students that the Grading Day and song announcements will be on Sunday instead of Monday the following week in an effort to crank up the pace. Darkness falls and the lads gather in the garden – Ainslie sporting a pair of devil horns given to him by trick or treaters at the Academy gates earlier – while Malachi proposes a moving toast to his fellow students as they watch fireworks exploding overhead.

KATIE THIS STUDENT NEEDS TO MOVE FORWARD. IN FACT, THIS STUDENT HAS RECEIVED THE SAME COMMENTS WEEK AFTER WEEK RICHARD

PIPPA JOINING KATIE IS A STUDENT WHO FINDS THEMSELVES A LITTLE WAY BEHIND. WE NEED TO FIND THE DYNAMICS OF THIS PERSON'S VOICE RICHARD

NIGEL THIS STUDENT WORKS HARD... THE ACADEMY NEEDS CLASS, QUALITY, AND IT NEEDS YOU PROVING THAT'S YOU RICHARD

ON PROBATION

Sing for Survival

LIVE SHOWDOWN DAY IS HERE YET AGAIN AND THE STUDENTS MAKE THEIR WAY TO SHEPPERTON STUDIOS. LEMAR REVEALS THAT HE COULD NEVER HAVE DREAMED HE WOULD ONE DAY BE PERFORMING WITH LIONEL RITCHIE. LIONEL, HOWEVER, CAN'T WAIT! "HE'S VERY COOL. WE'RE NOW RELAXED WITH EACH OTHER SO IT'LL BE A PIECE OF CAKE," THE MEGASTAR SAYS OF THEIR UPCOMING DUET.

With the Live Showdown just about to start, the studio is once again full of banners, and even Carrie has got one this week which claims: "Carrie rocks!" Sinead and Malachi's Irish fans are the loudest of the bunch as usual, but it's Cat's new fringe that attracts the most spontaneous "oohs".

Once the show kicks off, everyone takes their places and then the legend that is Lionel Ritchie takes a moment to give respect to the students. Soon it's time for the probationers to Sing For Survival. Pippa is up first and belts out Anastacia's "I'm Outta Love", closely watched by her parents and boyfriend Martin. A terrified looking Carrie watches her performance on a huge screen next to the stage, despite being just a few metres away from her. Pam is impressed and says "She did brilliantly," while Pippa looks even more nervous than before she sang.

Katie is next and sings Madonna's "Like a Prayer" as once again Carrie watches the monitor. Afterwards Kevin says that Katie is "Doing the biz", while Carrie disappoints the audience by saying that Katie needs a couple of years to reach her full potential, not a couple of weeks.

Finally it's Nigel's turn to Sing For Survival, and his rendition of Bryan Adam's "Heaven" wins praise from Pam who says he was "In Heaven tonight."

Richard sums up the three performances by saying he thought Nigel was best, whilst Katie has nudged Pippa out. But who will the public choose?

Ainslie and David take to the stage next to perform their Beatles number, "With A Little Help From My Friends", leaping down from the back of the set from 8 feet up. David jokingly strokes Ainslie's face when Cat announces they've paired up and despite the fact they didn't initially get on in the Academy, they jump around the stage like a couple of kids having a great time, then complete the song by pretending to fight, but hug instead.

It's Lionel's turn to say a few words next and he admits that if he had been in Fame Academy he may have been in trouble as the competition is so tough. He has some kind words for family man Nigel, who puffs his chest out with pride before leaning forwards to shake Lionel's hand. He also has some words of advice for all the students about the music business. "You have to love it. I still do it because I love doing it."

Marli and Malachi perform Sting's "Fields Of Gold" next and Carrie is full of praise, though she admits she thinks Malachi was better in rehearsals. Kevin nods in agreement as the audience boo.

After a long wait it's time for Lionel and Lemar's duet of 'Easy'. As the pair take to the stage, Lemar's parents look so proud they could burst and his mum stretches out her arms and gives him a big thumbs up. As soon as Lemar starts singing his mum's tears start flowing, and the duo give a breathtaking performance. Afterwards the crowd go wild and a beaming Kevin gives them a well-deserved standing ovation. The final performance of the night is from Grade A student Sinead, who sings Avril Levigne's 'Complicated'. Her cracking rendition prompts Richard to declare: "Sinead deserves to be Grade A again."

With the singing over it's time to find out who has won the public vote. Cat and Patrick build the suspense before revealing that Nigel has won with 56% of the vote and his wife gets to her feet and cries tears of joy. Next it's time for the students' vote and as Pippa and Katie hug and try to look brave, Pippa's bottom lip starts to tremble. But despite her obvious panic, she takes it surprisingly well when Katie pips her at the post. "I'm off to have a pint!" Pippa grins after hugging her fellow students. And with that she runs off stage and into the arms of her dad.

Back at the Academy, the surviving students have a celebratory drink. Malachi takes a stroll in the grounds with Jeremy and admits that Carrie's comments about his performance have left him feeling deflated. He also reveals that he feels that he should have been on probation this week and is hoping he is put on probation the following week. Time will tell.

FUNKY WHITE DIVA PIPPA IS THE FOURTH STUDENT TO BE EVICTED FROM FAME ACADEMY. BUT SHE'S NOT BITTER, BECAUSE DESPITE THE HEAD'S COMMENTS MAKING HER ANGRY AND KEVIN'S DANCE CLASSES NEARLY MAKING HER CRY, SHE ABSOLUTELY LOVED HER TIME IN FAME ACADEMY.

How do you feel about being expelled?

I'm completely fine with it. I knew I was going to have to come out one week and I said to myself that any time after the first week is a complete bonus. I've had the best time there. I think I've come out at a good time as it wasn't in the first week and it wasn't right near the end, so I wasn't too close to the prize.

Did you expect to go?

To be honest, every week I was on probation I prepared myself for going home.

Are you annoyed with the students that didn't vote for you?

Not at all, no. You can't be best chums with everyone in there and people are going to have their favourites. When I was on probation in the first week Ainslie said he was really sorry he didn't vote for me, but I was completely cool with it. You just forget about it after a while.

Why do you think Nigel voted for Katie?

I don't know because they totally don't get on. Me and Nigel aren't like best friends, but I get on with him. Carrie reckons it was tactics. Maybe because we're from the same area he wanted to be the one who came out best out of us? Who knows, but I think it's going to get even more tactical from now on.

How nervous were you standing up there waiting to hear the student votes?

I was pretty nervous. Nigel had the deciding vote and it was brilliant because when it went round to him the whole audience was shouting: "Pippa". It was so cool.

You seemed to take the news you were going really well...

Everyone was saying that I put on a brave face, but that was genuinely how I felt because I was really looking forward to seeing my family and friends. Everybody's got to go through it and crying and being bitter won't get you anywhere. We all read the rules and we all knew the situation. I saw Marli talking on the show last night about being on probation and she was making excuses about it and you can't do that because it makes you look silly.

What was the first thing you did when you left?

My dad ran up the stairs to the stage and I hugged him for ages and I cried. I think it was

just a cry of relief. People don't realise how stressful it is in Fame Academy. You're on an emotional roller-coaster. So it was so nice to see my family and then go back to the hotel for a pint. Not that I could drink. I think I've forgotten how to!

How was it seeing your boyfriend after all those weeks?

Oh, it was fantastic. I really, really, really missed him. I didn't really get to see him initially as I was doing interviews and stuff, but Kevin sneaked him into my BBC Choice interview so I got to give him a hug. Fame Academy was a big thing for me because I'd never lived outside Hull or away from home, and it was brilliant getting to see everyone again.

Is it weird being back in the real world?

Oh yeah. I've been in the Daily Mail in Hull every day, so I know that when I go home I'm going to get mobbed. I don't think I'm ever going to have a quiet life again. I've already been asked for my autograph in London loads and people have wound down their windows and shouted things like "You go girl!" at me. It's so weird because I forget I've been on TV!

Has anything you've watched on Fame Academy since you've been out surprised you?

I didn't realise that Ainslie was a bit nutty, because he's so all right usually. I know he likes having a laugh and things like that, but I thought that was just his mental sense of humour. I didn't know he talked to himself and talked to plants and stuff. That's really weird! I really like him, but he's very odd.

You got quite a lot of fan mail. What was the weirdest thing you got?

I got this one letter that had really scruffy writing and on one side it said, "Why does Pippa sing

so high?" and on the other side it says, "Why does Pippa wear so much make-up?" And I don't wear any! Everyone thought it was so funny.

Why do you think you kept getting put on probation?

I don't know. I've never thought I'd be famous or an artist and I'd never even had singing lessons before Fame Academy. I think because of that I only had one gear, which was fifth gear, and I used to belt everything out. I think that was a problem and also the teachers didn't think I'd found my style. But I know what I want it to be – I want to be a funky white diva and sing R'n'B and dance tracks. I remember roaring all day when I first got put on probation, but I don't think I cried much about it after that.

What was the worst criticism you got from the teachers?

Richard Park really upset me when he said at my last Live Showdown that I need to pull my socks up. I was like: "Hello, I don't think so. I was a bit nervous but there were people who were ten times worse than me." That really annoyed me.

Why did you decide to go in for Fame Academy?

It was my dad who pushed me to do it. He knows how lazy I am and he knows that I would probably have never done it myself because I've got this really defeatist attitude. But we did a daft little video in my living room and sent it in and I got called in for an audition. I got through the Manchester auditions and then got invited to the London ones, but I was sent home after the first day so I thought that was it. Then about two weeks later I got called back again and I got in. It was like a whirlwind.

Who were you closest to in the Academy?

At first it was Marli, but I got on with Sinead the best. We're both so normal and down to

earth and we've both got big families. And I was quite close to Lemar as well. The only people I would say I wasn't mega-close to were Nigel, Chris and Ashley. I really liked Katie, but she lets things get out of perspective and overreacts a bit. She had so much energy and would come and tickle you and stuff and it would drive you mad! She also really missed her family and she would get tearful quite often. It's a lot for her.

You've said before that every time In the Academy farted a lot. Who was the worst offender?

Malachi and Katie trumped a lot. Nigel also did and it really reeked and he had a bad habit of not admitting it. He once blocked a toilet with – you know – and Ainslie showed everybody and Nigel wouldn't admit it for ages. We wrote a little song to the melody of 'I'm Like a Bird' which went: "I'm Nigel's turd, I never flush away, I don't like to admit it'. Nigel would get really mad. Sometimes he could take a joke really well, but other times he'd get way defensive.

How's your leg after you hurt it in Kevin's dance class?

It's better, but it was so painful. I was walking really stupid for ages. Kevin's classes were so tough, it was like boot camp. I nearly cried so many times. Marli and I kept saying that one day we were just going to walk out. But the end results were brilliant so it was worth it.

Who do you think has a good chance of winning Fame Academy?

I think Lemar is the favourite to win, but I would like Sinead to win. But you never know because it's down to the public. I think the last three will be Lemar, Ainslie, and Sinead.

Who do you think will be the next out?

Well it's Marli, Malachi and Katie and I think that if Marli gets voted in by the public, Katie will go. And I reckon if the public votes Malachi in – if people are being tactical – they'll get rid of Marli because she's more of a threat.

Are you more or less determined to make it in music now?

Much, much more. I'll try anything. I've always been determined and now I've got to get my bum out of Hull and get out there.

I feel like I could do anything now. I'm really excited about some offers I've had because there's been some interest about my 'diva-ish' voice. Judge Jules's manager gave me his number yesterday and we're going to talk about some dance tracks. I'll keep at it and if nothing happens, fair enough, but I've had the best time.

Interview
Carrie

WE SPOKE TO VOCAL COACH CARRIE AFTER SHE'D SPENT A FEW WEEKS IN THE ACADEMY TO FIND OUT WHO SHE THINKS IS TOUGH ENOUGH TO SEE FAME ACADEMY THROUGH TO THE END.

How are you finding the Fame Academy experience?

I am loving it. It's the best job I've had in my whole life. It's totally exhausting and totally fabulous. It's absolutely full-on because there's a new show each week and the students have got all their emotional things going on, but it's great.

Can you talk us through one of your lessons...

My lessons are different every day, but my aim over the series is to find the students' musical identity. That's a really important thing. Sometimes I will steer them, but it's really about them coming up with their own ideas so they're singing around what their identity is.

Why do you think finding their identity is so important?

One of the things you have to think about a lot in the music business is how someone is going to market themselves. Their image, their singing and their music have all got to say the same thing. A record company have got to totally understand what someone is about because they've got to sell that to the public. If the artists don't know who they are then the record company may not know, and the public certainly won't know. My job is to help them to find who they are.

And how are you getting on?

Some people have got really definite ideas about who they are and others are less certain, so we're developing them. Most artists only use 50% of their voice and it's all about finding that other 50% that they're not using and encouraging them to be who they are.

Who do you think is showing the most promise?

Someone like Camilla shows great promise and Lemar shows amazing potential. I think he could be a world class R'n'B soul singer. I think Ainslie shows great potential and so does Sinead. And I've seen great potential in David as well. They've all got something, but it depends what market you're going for. For instance, housewives will love Nigel and he's got a great voice, so he could bring out an album of rock covers and do really well. But I'm not sure if that's what Fame Academy is looking for. But that's only my opinion.

We're a few weeks into the show. Who do you think has changed most?

I think the biggest shock for me was David because it wasn't until two days ago that he finally admitted he could songwrite. I was like: "Hello! This isn't a holiday camp. You can't sit here for two weeks and not mention this!" Pam said he was a good songwriter but she didn't rave so I just thought he would be quite good. It wasn't until he played me his songs that I realised he's amazing. So I've totally changed my mind about David, but he has got to keep proving himself. I also think Pippa is really coming on.

But she keeps getting put on probation...

Yes, but we have to look at the whole picture. She has come on the most, but if I took her and Sinead to a record company, who would be the long-term artist? For me, it would be Sinead.

So you think Sinead has a good chance of making it big?

It's funny with Sinead. I love her, I'm a big fan, but I find that people either love her or hate her. There's no in between with Sinead and it's really interesting. All the canteen staff here absolutely love her, but then other people say to me they can't stand her because she's always moaning. I think she's got an incredible voice and she's very talented and she's her own person. She hasn't mixed in as well as others, but she also holds her own.

So Sinead is keeping it real, but who's playing up for the cameras?

Oh, they all are. Marli has been massively, as have Nigel and Ainslie. I think they think they're on a sitcom! They're doing dramatic pauses and stuff. There's nothing wrong with playing up to the cameras a bit, though. Although Ainslie has whole conversations with himself in a room knowing full well that the cameras are watching him.

Do you think it's hard for the students having the cameras on them all the time?

It is but they're getting more used to it. It's hard because in Kevin's classes the cameras are hidden, but in my classes you've got cameramen so it's hard to ignore them. We had an incident a couple of weeks ago where a cameraman fell backwards though a cupboard and it made the most almighty crash. We tried to carry on as if nothing has happened, but in the end we all started laughing while this poor guy lay there with a camera on top of him.

What tips would you give to someone who's trying to get into the music business?

It's all about identity, identity, identity. That's the main thing. You have to have your unique selling point. This industry is about creativity, but you've also got to find a place where you can be marketed. You have to think about how you can be marketed and how you can sell yourself. You have to develop yourself in your own mind and the music that you like, your image and, of course, your voice. Those three things have to work together.

Can you give us an example of someone who it works perfectly for?

If you look at Robbie, he was so unhappy in Take That, but he was always Robbie. He was always a complete star, just an unhappy one. It was

only when he changed his image and started getting tattoos and looking more like a rocker that his music became more rocky and it worked with his personality. And his voice works with it as well, so you kind of go: "Ah, that makes sense now." You can't fit a round peg into a square hole and I think that if you try to do that the artist is going to be very unhappy. You can get away with it if you're in the manufactured side of the industry, but that only lasts a couple of years. If you're faking it you'll have a couple of albums and then it's all over.

Do the boys in the Academy flirt with you?
Yes, they do a bit. They'll do it when they're in a group, but sometimes when they're on their own they get very bashful.

Who is the worst flirt?
It has to be Malachi. But he'll flirt with anything, even the statues, so I can't get much kudos from him flirting with me. Malachi is lovely, though. He's such a fun guy. Chris was a flirt too. He was giving it all with the eyes.

Who do you think is going to win Fame Academy?
I think at the moment there are three people who could possibly win; Lemar, Ainslie or David. That's if I'm guessing who the public will go for, as they do tend to vote for guys. I think Sinead is very talented and I think Marli has talent, but she's let her personal life come into her artistic life a lot so at the moment she's not shining. It remains to be seen how she will do for the rest of the series.

Do you think we could all be totally surprised by the winner, though?
Anything is possible. The more I keep saying that Nigel should be on probation, the more the public are going to say: "We hate that vocal coach, let's vote for Nigel!" So he could end up

winning. He's the housewife's choice. He's the kind of artist who would have one TV advertised hit album, but we're not looking for one album. Nigel could do cabaret for the rest of his life and make a nice living out of it and good luck to him. But for me, that's not what Fame Academy is about. For me Fame Academy is about finding a long term creative artist that the business can have respect for. The thing is Nigel wants to be Robbie Williams and I don't think that's going to happen. I may sound harsh, but he's going to be out in front of record companies in however many weeks time and that's what they're going to be saying to him, so he might as well hear it now.

Week Five

Saturday

The students open their fan mail over breakfast. Lemar is disappointed not to have received any, but is amused when Malachi reads out an adoring ditty a female fan has sent him. The students watch their performances from the previous night's Live Showdown and Carrie has nothing but praise for Katie, Lemar, Sinead, Ainslie and David's performances. However, Carrie tells Malachi that he needs to smile more and announces: "You look like a mad axe murderer!"

Katie gets praise in her vocal lesson: "You're progressing each week. If I were you I'd be so proud of myself." Katie agrees and says that she was really pleased with last night's performance.

In the afternoon, Pam asks the students to pair off and try to write a hit love song. A few hours later it's David and Katie's track, 'Kiss These Tears Away', that stands out most, but she isn't overly impressed with any of the love ditties and accuses the students of being uninspired. Their efforts are rewarded, however, with the girls receiving cosmetics and cocktails and the boys getting beer. Over dinner, Katie is upset when Nigel announces that Carrie has, in a round about way, accused him of tactical voting and inferred that he voted Pippa out because she is the stronger student. Katie is upset and vows to confront Carrie about it the following day.

The early evening is spent singing love songs and there appears to be a spark of romance between Sinead and Malachi. First Malachi dedicates The Pogues' 'A Rainy Night in Soho' to the object of his affections, then looks on longingly as she sings the Tracy Chapman classic 'Baby Can I Hold You'. They round the evening off by singing a duet of a track called 'I Hope I Don't Fall In Love With You', before kissing each other on the cheek. Woo hoo!

Later on, the students are ushered to the dance studio to find that it's been given a romantic restaurant theme with sexy low lighting and champagne. The group pair off – Lemar with Marli, Sinead with Nigel, Katie and Malachi, and Ainslie and David – and share a dinner before the slow dancing starts. However, at least for tonight, there is no snogging.

Sunday

The rib that Ainslie hurt during his wrestling match with Malachi is cause for concern during the dance class and Kevin suggests he see the doctor again. Nigel is also in the wars having injured his foot.

The students are each given a plant to match their personalities. Marli is touched when Richard says she has been given an orchid for her "exotic personality and looks." Ainslie is ecstatic with his Yukka and spends time chatting with it in the greenhouse as soon as he gets a chance. The teachers meet and praise Lemar, Sinead, Malachi and Nigel but they are unimpressed with Marli's "okay" performance the previous Friday.

Pam admits she is worried about how the students' songwriting is going and says she thinks the problem is to do with scheduling: "They need to get a block of time where they can concentrate fully on songwriting." Sinead and Malachi's flirting continues as they read some of their fan letters. "Malachi, everyone thinks you and me should get it on," Sinead tells her Irish pal. After telling her he had given her every opportunity to make a move the night before, Malachi asks Sinead if she would go for it if the cameras weren't there. "I might do Malachi. I don't like giving you a straight answer!" she teases.

Jeremy challenges the students to make a Bonfire Guy from a collection of bad wigs and even worse clothes. There is much laughter from the students as they try on said garments and pretend to be an array of bizarre people, before finally creating their Guy.

Monday

A twitchy Nigel is dismayed to find that there are no spoons for him to eat his morning cereal. After repeating the word "spoons" to himself

several times, he tells everyone: "I want spoons, I want spoons!" Eventually Malachi hits breaking point and tells a shocked Nigel to "Shut up!"

David is ecstatic when he discovers that he's this week's Grade A student. But Marli is gutted when she discovers that she's on probation alongside Katie and Malachi. "I'm really shocked!" an emotional Marli confides to Ainslie, who responds: "You'll be fine. You'll totally cruise it". Malachi and Ainslie go outside for a chat about Malachi's probation and Ainslie tells him: "I know that the first couple of weeks we misbehaved big time and I think we should continue that. But maybe some of the energy should also go towards working to keep us both in."

David is chuffed to hear he'll be performing one of his own tracks on Friday night. Ainslie admits to Jeremy that he'll vote for Malachi regardless on Friday: "If Malachi goes I will be absolutely gutted. It'll completely change the whole experience for me – more than anything has changed it since I arrived." He also says he isn't happy about his duet with Nigel and would much rather be paired up with Lemar.

Marli talks to Jeremy about how unhappy she is about being on probation, and says that she plans to get very naughty and may even streak around the Academy. Watch this space…

Pam is furious when Ainslie arrives five minutes late for her class and asks him: "Would you be late for Carrie or Kevin's class, Ainslie? Please show me the same respect." She chastises the group, telling them: "I need hits. Do you want to record one of your own songs and have it released on record? Yes."

The students are treated to fireworks and throw their much-loved Guy George Hathaway – whom they have named after the Academy ghost – on to the fire. Marli lives up to her promise of being more sexy when she and Ainslie strip down to their underwear and have a mud fight. After rolling around in the freezing, slimy muck for several minutes Nigel declares them "proper mental". He's not kidding.

Tuesday

The students are extremely excited to discover that international superstar Mariah Carey will be taking their Masterclass later in the day. There's even more excitement for David when he discovers that his Grade A prize is an outing to watch the Worthington Cup game between Arsenal and Sunderland at Highbury. Not only that, but he and his chosen guest – Nigel – will be seated in the executive suite and meet Arsenal midfielder Giovanni Van Bronckhorst, who used to play for David's beloved Glasgow Rangers.

Ainslie, Malachi and Lemar have a mad songwriting session in the garden and come up with a ditty about a butcher who murders his customers, whilst mimicking some of the teachers' comments about their past performances.

David runs through 'Living The Lie', the self-penned track he will perform on Friday. "It's about, stop pretending that things aren't there when they are. Go and do something about it!" he explains to Carrie. Nigel, Ainslie and Malachi are summoned to the Head's office for their half term report. Richard grills Ainslie about whether he thinks Malachi has got what it takes and Ainslie doesn't hesitate before saying a defiant "Yes".

Mariah Carey arrives at the Academy and the boys all admit they're going to try and take a peek at her cleavage during the Masterclass. Each student sings for Mariah individually so she can suss out their voices and after trying out backing vocals for Mariah's new single, the braver ones get the chance to sing it for real. "Keep it real light and whispery; I don't know what you're doing but I love it!" an impressed Mariah tells a slightly worried looking Marli as she takes to the mike. Finally the students are split into two groups of girls and boys and both get to sing backing vocals for 'Through The Rain'. Then in a flurry of flowers Mariah is gone, but not before telling the students: "You guys were amazing. Good luck. Kisses to all of you and take care!"

KATIE **THERE IS STILL A LOT OF WORK TO BE DONE** RICHARD

MARLI **UNDERPERFORMED SINCE SHE MADE GRADE A** KEVIN

MALACHI **PEAKED TOO EARLY IN REHEARSALS** KEVIN

ON PROBATION

DAVID

DAVID HAS
OVERTAKEN A LOT
OF THE OTHERS
PAM

GRADE A

wednesday

Jeremy holds a controversial PDP where each person has to write a positive and negative comment about each of the other students and stick it on their backs. Despite being labelled "caring, very sexy and fun", the session leaves Marli in tears after she is also deemed "manipulative, unfaithful and disloyal." Malachi comes off best and is described as "funny, sensitive and charming". After the session the students rally round a sobbing Marli and offer words of comfort. Ainslie and Malachi have a discussion in the garden about who would have written the unkind comments, with neither of them claiming responsibility.

Malachi impresses Carrie during his rehearsal, although she emphasises that he needs to put more personality into his performance. He blames his lack of dancing skills for his shyness, but is told: "You do know the industry is not about dancing, it's about performing. There's a real charm about you. You've got to charm the pants off Britain." Sinead beware!

Nigel and Ainslie practise their Showdown duet, but Nigel is having serious problems remembering the words. Malachi and Sinead flirt with each other in the lounge, which results in Malachi passing Sinead a note declaring: "'My dearest Sinead. I wish you all the luck today, tomorrow.... I love you from the bottom of my heart." Nigel and David head off to the football, with a grinning David telling the others: "It's nearly time for football, beer and a pie. Woo hoo! The outside world! Oh man this is going to be wicked."

Marli tells Katie that she feels the students are becoming more competitive and as she contemplates Friday's Showdown, she thinks she will be expelled and likens Fame Academy to a battle.

There are smiles all round when Lemar announces he is now Uncle Lemar: his brother has become the proud father of a baby boy. The champagne is cracked open once again and Sinead plays congratulations on her guitar as the others sing along. A tipsy Ainslie tries to whip his Irish buddy with a bunch of roses, but Malachi isn't having any of it and flees the scene before things get painful. The drunken boys arrive back and Nigel excitedly tells everyone about how he's been signing autographs all night.

Thursday

With the 50th anniversary of the Singles Charts just around the corner, the students are given three choices of past number ones and asked to choose one to perform on a special Number Ones show. Malachi plumps for Don McLean's 'Vincent', Sinead chooses No Doubt's 'Don't Speak', Lemar goes for Bryan Adams's 'Everything I Do', Katie picks Madonna's 'Papa Don't Preach', Marli goes for Sinead O'Conner's 'Nothing Compares 2 U', Nigel's favourite is Chicago's 'If You Leave Me Now', while David is more than happy with his choice of Wet Wet Wet's 'Goodnight Girl'.

Kevin, Carrie and Richard have a chat about the students before tomorrow's Live Final and all agree that Marli, Malachi and Katie should put in good performances. They are less confident about Ainslie and Nigel, feeling that their duet is defeating them somewhat. A hungover David struggles through Kevin's dance class, but it's Kevin who's left stuck for words when Carrie confronts him about going to the match with David and Nigel, despite the fact he hates football. "I am a lifelong Arsenal fan and you went to the football without telling me you were going," Carrie rants. "Not only that – students hear this – Kevin got back last night and didn't have his mic on!" Oops.

The first ever Fame Academy awards ceremony takes place on Saturday over a five star meal in the ballroom. Richard announces to the students that they will each be given a nomination form to vote in a variety of categories. Richard reveals that David's song, Living The Lie, has been played on the radio, and also tells the students that Mariah Carey was so impressed she's requested that they sing with her at Friday's Live Showdown.

It's time for the probationers to give their survival speeches. Old hand Katie steps up first and says: "Thanks for voting me in the last three times, it's given me a chance to prove myself and I now feel I'm growing as an artist." Next it's Malachi's turn. "I'm not going to beg, thanks everyone for the experience. I've worked with the best; I've had a brilliant and lovely time I'll always cherish." And finally Marli takes her place in front of the group. "I feel like I haven't fulfilled myself yet. I'll be gutted to leave. You guys blow me away and I'm going to cry, and thank you."

Sing for Survival

IT'S TIME FOR THE LIVE SHOWDOWN, AND KATIE CAN'T STOP SMILING BECAUSE SHE'S BEEN SENT FOWERS BY HER LOCAL NEWSPAPER. AS THE AFTERNOON GOES ON, THOUGH, THE SMILES FADE AND THE NERVES START TO KICK IN. AFTER A LENGTHY REHEARSAL AT SHEPPERTON STUDIOS, THE STUDENTS DON THEIR GLAD RAGS AND PREPARE TO FACE THE PUBLIC.

After weeks of coming to the show, it seems the parents are getting to know each other pretty well and Katie's mum gives Lemar's mum a big cuddle before the show starts. There are loads of banners for Marli, and lots of support for Malachi whose fans are without a doubt the most vocal.

With just minutes to go, the students and teachers take their seats. Superstar Mariah Carey slinks in just behind them and the audience go crazy. She's certainly taken a shine to Lemar, and as the audience cheer and shout in her direction, she gives them a delicate wave whilst wrapping her other arm around Lemar's shoulders.

The show soon kicks off and Marli is first to Sing For Survival. She gives a flawless interpretation of Smokey Robinson and The Miracles' 'Tracks Of My Tears' which prompts Kevin to claim: "She's back!" and Carrie to comment: "I think Marli has great identity. You know in the first few notes that's Marli." Even Marli herself admits: "Probation was the best thing for me. I'm back."

It's Malachi's turn to show what he can do, and it's obvious he's been listening to the teachers' advice as he belts out a very animated rendition of David Gray's 'Babylon'. "We've been waiting for him to smile for five weeks, and tonight he finally did!" a relieved Carrie grinned. However, Pam added: "He still has the potential to improve on his performances."

Katie is the last of the probationers to strut her stuff, and gives a feisty performance of Fairground Attraction's 'Perfect', with her pal Sinead dancing along. An impressed Carrie thinks it's one of her finest offerings to date, and says: "She's got the performance, we have to find the identity... tonight she was great!" Richard names Malachi as best, Marli as second best, and poor Katie last in his order or personal preference for the evening.

It's the turn of the non-probationers to show that they can do, and Sinead and Lemar are up first with a sexy rendition of U2's 'Still Haven't Found What I'm Looking For'. They round the song off with a hug, but afterwards Carrie criticises Sinead's timing.

Mariah Carey is set to sing next, but before she does she has some words of wisdom for the students: "Be passionate and love it more than anything. Roll with the punches," she declares. She certainly does a passionate version of her single 'Through The Rain', with the eager students impressing everyone on backing vocals.

Nigel and Ainslie manage to put their differences aside to team up for their duet of Sting's 'Every Little Thing She Does Is Magic'. They wow everyone as they rise up from beneath the stage on chairs before launching into action. But Carrie still isn't convinced that Nigel has found his identity. The final performance is from Grade A student David, who gets to sing his own track, Living The Lie. The teachers are quick to praise him. "Good strong chorus, great storyline," says Pam, while Carrie smiles: "I think the next thing David should do is prepare an album-full of material, because he'll need it."

The teachers round up the night and give their opinions of the best and worst performances, and it's not Perfect news for Katie.

	BEST	WORST
RICHARD	AINSLIE/DAVID	KATIE
PAM	LEMAR	KATIE
KEVIN	AINSLIE	KATIE
CARRIE	LEMAR	KATIE

The results of the phone vote are in, and despite the teachers being unimpressed with her efforts, Katie has won over the public with 47% of the votes. So it's now up to the students to decide between Marli and Malachi. The pair hug on stage as the students write down the name of who they want to save. But it's hard for the audience to concentrate on what's going on as Ainslie has positioned himself so far forward on his stool that his backside is hanging out of the back of his trousers, which is rather distracting for all of those behind him!

With the student votes counted and not one for poor Marli, it's obvious that she's on her way home. But she takes it gracefully, telling everyone: "I love these guys. I'm actually glad it's me leaving. I'm going to miss them all. Be naughty but be nice. Keep going, and I'll see you all when you get out." What a trooper.

Interview
Marli

MARVELLOUS MARLI IS FEELING FINE ABOUT BEING EXPELLED BECAUSE IT SAVED HER FROM HAVING TO RUN NAKED AROUND THE ACADEMY! STILL, NOTHING COULD HAVE TOPPED THAT SEMI-NAKED MUD WRESTLING...

How do you feel about being expelled?
I feel totally fine about it. I was definitely ready. And it's quite a relief being out, although it was quite a shock at first.

Do you wish you could have seen it through to the end?
I was hoping I would get down to the last four, but I think I would have got a lot wilder if I'd stayed in, so it's probably a good thing that I went. David and I were planning to streak round the whole Academy naked.

What do you consider your wildest moment in the Academy?
The stripping and the mud wrestling. I just thought, why not do it? One way of letting out my frustration in there was to be a bit naughty. Something was building up inside me and the mud wrestling seemed like the best thing to do. The mud looked like chocolate and I wanted to roll in it, so I did!

Were you conscious of the fact that people were watching you all the time?
No, otherwise I wouldn't have done half the things I did because I would have been thinking about my family. But they've actually been really good about it. My mum's like: "If you've got it, flaunt it!"

Fame Academy seemed to be a bit of an emotional rollercoaster for you...
I had a lot of personal things going on that I couldn't deal with. That's what was really getting me down. I couldn't pick up the phone and sort things out, so they were weighing on my mind the whole time. The pressure of having to do performances and everything with the baggage hanging over me started to get me down.

Did you expect to be expelled?
I knew the minute I got put on probation that I'd be out. That's why I cried, because I knew it was my last week. And when I got voted off I cried tears of relief because I knew it was going to happen.

Do you think you deserved to go, based on your performance?
Actually yes, I didn't think I did that great on the Friday. Maybe that's because mentally I knew I would probably be going. But based on previous performances and how much more I had to give, I don't think I should have gone.

Were you disappointed with any of the students who didn't vote for you?
Yes, Katie. Well not disappointed, but surprised. She was devastated and said that she wanted to rub what she wrote off and start again. She felt really bad, bless her, and I don't want her to. I said before I went on the show that Friday that the worst thing that could happen would be not to get one vote – and it did happen! But I told everyone not to worry. I could see their faces and Ainslie knew

that what he was doing was so wrong. He was keeping Malachi purely because he makes him laugh, but it doesn't matter at all.

What was the first thing you did when you left the stage?
I hugged my mum and dad and I had a pint of Guinness. They had one waiting for me and it was bliss. I really wanted to down it but I was worried about what they might think!

Did you miss your parents when you were in the Academy?
No, because I knew I would see them when I got out. But I did miss TV, and not being able to pick up the phone and deal with issues and call my friends for a moan. I couldn't deal with my baggage because I couldn't speak to anyone. I think that if I hadn't had the baggage, things would have been very different.

You had some love issues in the Academy and ended up splitting up with your boyfriend. How is everything now?
That's what really brought me down, to be honest. When I kissed Chris it made me feel so guilty and I hated myself afterwards.

I'd been seeing a guy for a month and I kept thinking about him and didn't want to do certain things because of him. That's the whole reason I left the six year relationship I was in before and I didn't want to have to go through it all again. I needed to be focused on myself and not have to think about anyone else. All of that was horrible because I wasn't able to sit down and talk to him about it. It all happened in a three minute phone call.

Have you seen him since you've been out?
No, but I will do. He's very understanding. He knows how hard I've worked to get here. I've been in the music industry for seven years and I've worked too hard to let it all slip for a relationship.

Did you fancy Chris or was the snog just a laugh?
It was just a bit of a game. He's really cute, but afterwards I felt really bad about what people would think.

Did any of the guys take your fancy?
Ainslie, he's lovely. I love Ainslie, I thought he was a star. I knew he'd get all the girls going. But I think he needs to get out now because he's showing sides of himself that he doesn't want to show. I think he's got to be careful.

What's your take on the Sinead and Malachi snog situation?
I was shocked because Sinead keeps herself to herself and was saying to us that she doesn't like Malachi and nothing was going to happen.

I actually thought something was going to happen between her and Ainslie. I don't know if she snogged Malachi for the camera or if it's part of her tactics or if it's genuine. It's mad. Malachi is really genuine and I think he likes her, so if she does genuinely like him, I think something else could happen between them.

And Katie has that big old crush on Kevin...

It's fun to have crushes in there. Sometimes there was nothing to do, and it was nice to have little fantasies. Katie and I even had a code in the Academy for when we really wanted to pounce on someone. It was a bit of a release. I liked someone in there too, but I'm not saying who.

No need to, we already know it's Jeremy!

Aaaaahhhhhh! How do you know? Aaahhhhhhh!

Do you regret anything you did in the Academy?

No, because I look back on it and I think: "I made good tv!" I was me. I laughed when I was happy and I cried when I was moody or I felt crap.

Do you think being Grade A in the first week was a bad thing as the only way was down?

Definitely, it was like I had nowhere else to go. I peaked too soon.

Who do you think plays up to the cameras in the Academy?

I think Ainslie is starting to now because he's going a bit barmy. Nigel does a bit as well and I think Sinead is being quite sneaky. I think she really wants to win it and is definitely playing the game.

Do you think the tactical voting has kicked in?

Absolutely. Big time. It'll be interesting to see how people play the game from now on.

How did you find the Fame Academy teachers?

Brilliant, but I think Richard should have been meaner. But I loved all of them, I think they're fantastic. I have so much respect for them.

What was your favourite class?

Kevin's workouts. I'd hate it – especially the jumps – but I'd feel great afterwards. His classes are the ones I miss most.

Who do you think will be out next between Nigel, Malachi and Katie?

I think Katie could be out this week, I think Nigel will get the public vote as he got 56% last time. I would actually like to see Nigel win as it would be two fingers up to all the people in the music industry who think you're past it after a certain age.

Who do you think is going to win?

I hope David does. He's a lovely, lovely, lovely bloke.

Who do you think will be the biggest star?

Lemar. He's fantastic.

You've had two record deals before; are you hoping it's going to be third time lucky?

Totally. I'm hoping that this is my big chance. I've been given a platform to launch myself from and I'm going to carry on writing and try to get that one hit. I've got about 60 songs in the bag that are great, but I need that one smash. I want to make sure everything is perfect.

Interview
Kevin

How's Fame Academy going for you?
I'm really, really enjoying it. It started off really well and it's been more hectic than I could ever have dreamed. But I'm absolutely loving it.

What are you enjoying most?
The results we're getting. Every Friday I look at the show and think we've moved on from last week. It's hard for people to be here in this environment and deliver well each Friday. It's a lot of pressure.

Who were you worried wouldn't be able to cut it dancing wise when you first met the students?
Nigel is really good and towards the end of week two he performed a dance routine with two other people that I picked out to be the best in the class. That would never have happened in the beginning. He hated the dancing and didn't understand why he had to do it, but now he's hardworking and determined and really, really moving on. And Malachi, bless him. When he danced on TV when he performed 'Sex Bomb' I was so happy because he was the centre of attention and it showed me how much he's moved on.

Who is your hot tip to win?
I would have said Ainslie, but we've got a few dark horses in the Academy. Marli was a hot contender but she slipped down a bit, so she needs to crawl back to the top of pile. David is doing really, really well and Pippa is moving onwards and upwards. Lemar is up there as a

front runner as well. It's not a foregone conclusion who is going to win, though, even if the students kind of think it is. People pull out some stunning performances on the Friday shows, so you never know.

Who do you think could go on to be the biggest star?
Lemar or Ainslie. And Malachi really isn't far behind because he's such a charmer and he's got a great voice. People forget about Malachi's voice because they always see him as the funny, charming guy, but he's great.

Who do you think would love the pop star lifestyle most?
Being a pop star, Pippa. Being a quirky star, Ainslie. Being a soul star, Lemar. And if she can get herself back to where she was, Marli.

Is there anyone in the Academy you don't think is cut out for pop stardom?
No, because I'm sure at some point in a lot of performers' careers you've thought that they weren't cut out for pop stardom. Look at Robbie Williams when he left Take That. Everyone said he was just a fat dancer from Take That and that Gary Barlow was the one who'd make it. But people have had to eat their words.

How do you feel about Katie fancying you?
I think it's funny because she hasn't even made eye contact with me. She's absolutely lovely but I'm engaged and I've got a baby on the way. And even though it's flattering to me, it's not very flattering to my pregnant girlfriend! I think Katie

is moving on to David now, so it will be really interesting to see how that develops. You miss your other halves while you're in here and the students have no contact with the outside world, so they're forging friendships and alliances. Sometimes that turns into love, infatuation, or whatever you want to call it, so we'll see how the relationships evolve.

Have the other girls flirted with you at all?
Yeah, every now and again. It's fun and they know it's going nowhere.

Can you see any other romances blossoming in the Academy?
I think Ainslie and Marli might have something going, but Marli is kind of closing up now because she's worried about how she'll be perceived in the outside world, which shouldn't be an issue. She's got a boyfriend out there as well and that always seems to be an issue when she talks about how she's being perceived.

What about Lemar and Camilla? They seem very close...
They are very touchy feely. Camilla says that they're just good friends, but I think it's more than that.

Do you feel bad when you upset people in your dance classes?
Why should I feel bad? I'm helping them to move on. If I upset someone and there was no progression I would be very upset. For instance, if I upset Ainslie and he left my class because of something I said without understanding why I said it and it didn't help him progress, that would bother me. I don't say things to upset people. At the end of the day I'm not 16 in the playground and I know that wouldn't achieve anything. In the next class they would come along and hate me and not respect me. I don't

give a flying whatever what they think about me, I'm just trying to help them.

Right, let's run through the students and you can tell me how you think they're getting on at the moment and what they'll do when they leave the Academy...

Ainslie – He has his own style and moves, and he's a great little dancer. He will do amazingly well. He reminds me of Michael Stipe from REM. He has a quirky character and has the ability to capture a moment and make you want to cry. He sang a couple of his own songs during the auditions and they were great. He has great potential and will have hit albums.

Malachi – When I first met Malachi I thought: "God, what have I done to deserve this?" But he does try and he's come on in leaps and bounds. I think he has a lot of potential. He's not a great dancer, but he makes me laugh and keeps me entertained and that's a great quality to have.

Marli – Marli started out as the one who would stick in my brain because she's really, really sexy, but she's settled down a bit and is tucked in behind the leaders and I don't think she's going to pull out. She can dance and she's flexible, but she's not as ahead of the class as she was. But I still think she could become a Tori Amos style artist.

Pippa – She really surprised me because she was a dancer before she came into the Academy and I saw no sign of that. She must have left her talent behind. But now she's really coming on and I think she'll go on to be an Atomic Kitten style pop girl.

Katie – Katie has the potential to be so much but she isn't there. She's like a gangly Olive Oil when she's dancing, but she really tries. She's having a great time and in a year's time I think she'll be really happy. But I don't know if she'll be happy living at home or as an artist.

Nigel – Nigel will always work and entertain people. He will always do shows and will pack out local clubs. I have no fear about him having a big album and then touring constantly making money. He's a great, great performer and he's doing good with his dancing.

David – He came in late but he's overtaken some of the front runners. He's very talented and he's doing good. I think he could be a Ronan Keating style artist, although I think he wiped the floor with Ronan when he sang 'When You Say Nothing At All'.

Naomi – Naomi is a beautiful girl and she's got a really nice personality, but I'm not sure where she'll go. I didn't really see enough of her to know what she's capable of.

Lemar – He's the next Craig David, although I think he's even better. He deserves to be a global success and I think he will be. He's a really good dancer and can dance and sing at the same time, which is the trickiest thing in the world.

Chris – Chris has the potential to be the new Justin Timberlake if he could get his singing as good as his dancing. His singing is just slightly behind.

Ashley – He's a good-looking chap and he's got a good heart. My mum got all the people at her church to pray for him because he reads his bible every morning! If he doesn't do well as a singer, he could be a TV personality.

Camilla – She'll be around as an artist, songwriter, performer and cover girl for a long time. She's a beautiful girl inside and out, so I hope she does really well. She took a little while to get going with the dancing, but she's getting better and better.

Sinead – I think Sinead has got the most amazing voice and she'll go a long way as a singer songwriter. I know she'll do well. I just know it. We picked 12 people out of thousands and even if only five go the distance, we've done an incredible job. There's a lot of talent in the Academy.

Saturday

Kevin kicks off the day by giving Malachi and Katie a good ticking off for talking while Mariah Carey was performing last night. "You had your mic under your arm and you were talking. That made me look really bad," he rages. A treat is in store, however, as the students will be provided with dinner jackets and ball gowns for the first ever Academy awards this evening.

The teachers have a half term meeting to discuss the students' progress. Lemar and Sinead are praised, but there are concerns for Ainslie's behaviour. "You make it as a star, then you misbehave – not the other way round," says Jeremy. Jeremy also has some concerns for Nigel. "I hope he doesn't tip over the edge and become cocky and arrogant… I've seen a few instances of that."

Pam sets the students a songwriting task where they must write a song about another student in the Academy. Ainslie admits to Jeremy he feels awful about the way the voting went last night. "I hate the thought that people think I vote tactically. If it had been anyone but Malachi I'd have voted for Marli. She's got more talent than most of us. Next week, I'll be voting in the most talented person." The students perform for The Guardian newspaper rock critic Caroline O'Sullivan, who is hugely impressed with their efforts.

After an evening of wine, dance and song, David and Ainslie decide to finish up with a rousing game of – what else? – bottom whipping. Smoothie Malachi settles next to Sinead on her bed to tell her a story, but things get passionate when Sinead pulls the tipsy Irishman towards her and the pair snog for a whopping 36 seconds. But how will they feel about it in the morning?

Sunday

It's headaches and red faces all round as Katie remembers telling Kevin she fancies him. The Sinead/Malachi gossip soon spreads round the Academy, but Sinead tells Katie: "It was only a snog. We're not in love or anything. A bit of fun like", but admits to Ainslie that Malachi is a good snogger! Nigel has a few stern words with Katie about her behaviour towards Kevin. "Your boyfriend, he really loves you. Don't be mean to him while you're in here. I just think for your own benefit, you should control your feelings," he lectures. Katie sleeps off her hangover, but David is busy writing songs and admits to Nigel that his guitar is the only thing keeping him sane in the Academy, as he's beginning to really miss home, while Nigel reveals that he's desperate to be Grade A student. The students meet with the Academy styling team to try to create an image for themselves. Carrie gets the students thinking when she asks them: "I want to sell you to the marketplace. How do I advertise you?" Lemar settles on a David Beckham look, while the team reckon Malachi would suit a Guy Ritchie gangster style.

Monday

The three Grade A students are announced as Lemar, Sinead and Ainslie, all of whom will get to sing live on Chris Moyles' Radio One show for a chance to perform on Children In Need and become the Academy's first A+ student. The probationers are Malachi and Katie, with the third being announced on Wednesday. Neither David or Nigel are very happy about having to wait to discover their fate. Katie sheds a few tears, admitting: "I thought I wouldn't be bothered but I am. It's just getting me down now."

Malachi opens his heart to Pam about being on probation. He thinks he has a good chance of being expelled. Pam tells him: "You've got so much charisma, so much charm… I'd like to see you bring that on stage." Nigel chats to Ainslie about his period of writer's block but his mood doesn't improve as he throws a strop when he's cut off mid-sentence during his three minute phone call with his wife, Mel. He claims he didn't hear the ten second warning and

storms upstairs swearing, followed by a worried Jeremy. It's not just the phone call that's bothering Nigel: as well as not having been made Grade A, the threat of probation is looming. "It's like the hangman's noose – they're going to keep you there for three days. I just want to know".

Tuesday

Ainslie, Sinead and Lemar arrive at Radio One and back at the Academy David and Malachi are feeling very left out and write a song about being left behind.

Even so, it doesn't stop them huddling around the radio to hear Ainslie's take on Charles Aznavour's 'She', Sinead's version of 'Don't Speak' by No Doubt, and Lemar's rendition of Bryan Adams's '(Everything I do) I Do It For You'.

It's up to the public to decide who will get the chance to sing at Children In Need on Friday and the trio make their way back to the Academy to gather around the radio to hear the results of the poll. Sinead is the clear winner with 48% of the votes and gets a hug from gracious loser Ainslie and a kiss on the cheek from Malachi.

On Ainslie's favourite bench outside, Katie sobs as she's missing home and her old chum Marli. "I just feel like there's no-one I'm close to. I feel like s**t," she sniffs, obviously still feeling guilty at having voted against her friend on last Friday's Live Showdown. "Don't cry. I hate seeing girls cry," says the sensitive Scotsman. Nigel wins a 15-minute phone call home after beating Katie in a block building game. At last, the Scunthorpe crooner has something to smile about! But things go from good to plain annoying when Malachi keeps Nigel up by repeatedly playing the word "Nigel" to him on his voice recorder. Nigel is less than impressed and lands a few punches on the cheeky Irish chap.

Wednesday

Malachi awakes to find that he has a black eye courtesy of Nigel's fist and is generally feeling a bit under the weather. Kevin suggests he takes a break, but he bravely battles on. Kevin has some sympathetic words for Katie who is still feeling down about being put on probation for the fifth time and the teachers' negative comments about her. "Craig David went to loads of record companies before he got signed, they said he was c**p. So people do get it wrong," says the sympathetic choreographer.

The students head off to Brent Cross to sing for cash for Children In Need, where a huge crowd has gathered to watch the students strut their stuff. Despite some initial disappointment at Lemar's absence due to illness, the audience go wild and wave banners and sing along as Sinead sings 'Ironic', Malachi croons 'Crazy Love' and Ainslie and Malachi and Sinead perform 'Keep Me a Secret'. David ups the tempo with 'Mustang Sally', Katie performs 'Perfect', while Nigel belts out 'Stuck In The Middle With You'. Several fantastic songs later the students raised bucketloads of cash, but we wonder if Marli, who was hiding in the audience in disguise, contributed? After many kisses have been handed out – mostly by Malachi – burly security guards escort the students out and they make their way back to the Academy.

Nigel is on a high after his 15-minute phone call to his wife and passes on some cheery secret info to his fellow students. "[Mel] said no matter what the teachers might say about you on the night, don't give it a second thought because none of you know what they say about you during the week." Wise words indeed!

Thursday

The teachers have a discussion about the students and admit that they still feel that Katie is lagging behind the others. They also agree that Ainslie has been hit hard by not winning the Radio One poll. Ainslie and Malachi argue after Ainslie accuses someone of stealing one of his CDs. Worried that he's pointing the finger at Sinead, Malachi leaps to her defence and the pair row. Nigel is disheartened after finding out that he is the third student up for probation this week and is particularly angry about the teachers' comments that he's yet to find his identity. Kevin grills the students about who they think will win Fame Academy and discovers that Lemar and Katie's money is on Ainslie, Ainslie thinks Lemar will clinch it and loyal Malachi is backing Sinead.

David and Ainslie have the time of their lives in Fame Academy's recording studio, laying down The Beatles classic 'With a Little Help From My Friends'. Richard tells them that they will all be going along to Children In Need tomorrow. Katie only has one thing on her mind: "Will there be a proper bar with, like, lager and black and stuff? Will I have to drink wine and champagne or can I drink lager and black?" The probationers make their speeches to their fellow students. Malachi keeps his short and sharp, claiming: "I want to stay here." Katie says: "It's been quite stressful for me and without your help I don't think I could have made it through." While Nigel thanks the fans, sings Katie's praises and wishes his mum a happy birthday. Ainslie and Malachi have a heart to heart, with a concerned Malachi telling Ainslie that he doesn't think he's been himself for the past few days. "I'm too paranoid a person to be on a reality TV show. I think everyone hates me!" comes Ainslie's maudlin reply.

Friday

Sinead leaves the Academy at 7.00am to go to another Children In Need rehearsal. She arrives back looking tired at 10.00am and finds the other students preparing themselves for a big songwriting session. Malachi works on his track, 'Eyes Of Blue', which is written about a fellow student. He's not revealing which one, but the sensitive lyrics mean it's not too hard to work out that it's Sinead.

Although Sinead is looking gorgeous, she's very nervous and it takes Jeremy and Malachi to calm her down before she sets off for the show. When she does eventually take to the stage a little later than scheduled, she gives an amazing performance of 'Don't Speak', which leaves the audience in no doubt about how incredibly talented she is.

Her fellow students join her to hand over a cheque for a massive £40,000 that has been raised from the voting lines since the Academy opened its doors. Backstage all of the students take full advantage of the booze on offer. After arriving back to the Academy a little tipsy, they decided to hold the Academy's first ever wedding. Ainslie and Katie are bride and groom, Sinead grabs the best man slot, Nigel is the father of the bride, Lemar is the wedding singer, while Malachi

carries out the ceremony. The ring? A chocolate doughnut. Who said romance was dead?

Saturday

Sinead heads off to appear on The Saturday Show as part of her prize for being Grade A+ student while the other students get suited, booted and high-heeled for a photo shoot with OK! Magazine. Sinead is a total star on The Saturday Show, performing 'Don't Speak' once again.

Back at the Academy Katie is having a huge hair disaster while having her highlights done and enlists Richard's help to get something sorted out immediately.

The Head is also on hand to dish out some romance advice to Malachi. "Before long, you and Sinead will be on Mr and Mrs," he tells him as he takes a photo of the pair together on the sofa. Nigel throws a strop when the lights are turned out while he's trying to pack his suitcase in case he's expelled tomorrow night. He stomps down the stairs shouting and swearing. "It's supposed to be 'act like a four-year-old and be treated like a four-year-old'. Not 'be treated like a four-year-old and then act like one" he tells anyone who will listen. He appears to have got the acting part perfected!

Sunday

Probationers Nigel, Katie and Malachi are gearing up for the Live Showdown and have a discussion about the prospect of leaving the Academy. Let's get down to Shepperton Studios and find out who's going to be leaving tonight…

Fame Academy Award Winners

MOST LIKELY TO MAKE IT ▸ LEMAR
BEST SINGER ▸ LEMAR
TWO LEFT FEET ▸ MALACHI
BEST LOOKING BLOKE ▸ MALACHI
BEST SONGWRITER ▸ DAVID
TOUGHEST TEACHER ▸ KEVIN
THE BIGGEST MOANER ▸ AINSLIE
BIGGEST DRAMA QUEEN ▸ NIGEL
MOST SNOGGABLE TEACHER ▸ CARRIE
MOST GORGEOUS GIRL ▸ KATIE

KATIE **NEEDS TO WORK HARD ON COMMANDING THE STAGE**
RICHARD

MALACHI **DOESN'T HAVE THAT HUNGER FOR FAME**
CARRIE

NIGEL **WE STILL BELIEVE THIS PERSON HAS AN IDENTITY SEARCH**
RICHARD

ON PROBATION

Sing for Survival

THE NOISE LEVELS ARE RISING AND THINGS ARE JUST ABOUT TO KICK OFF DOWN AT SHEPPERTON STUDIOS. THE AUDIENCE IS ONE OF THE LOUDEST OF THE SERIES AND THE BIGGEST BANNER TO DATE – A HUGE GREEN OFFERING BEARING SINEAD'S NAME – IS BEING PROUDLY DISPLAYED WHILE DANAAN AND VANESSA FILM THE BBC CHOICE LINKS.

The teachers and students take up their usual positions and the three probationers walk slowly to the middle of the stage. As Cat and Patrick call out their names, the nerves appear to hit Katie and she looks terrified. Sinead waves furiously to family and friends, while Ainslie is lapping up all the attention he's getting from his female supporters. It's excitement all round as for the first time ever, all the students will be singing solo, performing their favourite number ones from years gone by.

Nigel is the first of the probationers to sing and tells Cat he's glad it was him and not David who was put on probation this week because: "He's a great guy and for the sake of his songwriting talent he needs to stay in the Academy." Cat is impressed with his gentlemanly behaviour and without further ado, he strides up the runway and breaks into Marvin Gaye's 'I Heard It Through The Grapevine'. Carrie thinks he did really well and says he did well to recover after a bad start to the song. Patrick asks Kevin if he thinks Nigel could have bettered his performance, to which his wife Mel cheekily shouts "No!"

Katie is next up and Cat asks her if she's ever felt like giving up during her Fame Academy probation journey. "No, it makes me stronger and makes me want to keep on going and get better," comes her reply. Katie launches into Madonna's 'Papa Don't Preach' and Sinead claps along. Carrie makes a few enemies in the audience when she says that Katie: "Still has a way to go."

Malachi is the final probationer to perform and Cat grills him about how he and Sinead are getting along. "We're both single and we had a bit of fun the other night," he smiles, staring directly at Sinead. He does a cracking rendition of Don McLean's 'Vincent' and the teachers watch the screens intently to see how he's coming across, while Ainslie looks on nervously. Carrie is clearly impressed and declares: "Malachi's performance was absolutely brilliant! I think he charmed his way through that." He's certainly a

smoothie: after greeting fans near him, he thanks the audience for their support and has them eating out of his hand. Patrick and Cat announce that the teachers will be naming the first of next week's probationers at the end of tonight's show: Ainslie looks furious while David gives a wry smile. It's David's turn to sing next and he croons Wet, Wet, Wet's ballad 'Goodnight Girl'. Carrie is pleased with his performance, but Pam thinks he should have done something "A little edgier." Long before Lemar takes to the stage to sing Bryan Adams's '(Everything I Do) I Do For You', his lovely mum is up cheering for him. He looks smooth in his snazzy white suit and sings brilliantly, but Jeremy insists that the competition isn't won yet!

Ainslie is raring to go and belts out Charles Aznavour's 'She'. Despite his bizarre neck attire, Carrie states that he's the strongest visual performer in the Academy, although she feels that he struggled tonight. But Kevin is hugely impressed, saying: "He has a strong identity and he can handle anything that's thrown at him and you need that in this business." Songbird Sinead is the final student to perform and storms through 'Don't Speak'. "She looks like a star!" says Carrie, to rapturous applause from the audience. Sinead confesses to Cat that things are getting more competitive in the Academy and Jeremy admits that Sinead's self-contained personality scared him when they first met, but he now thinks she's genuine and sincere. The teachers choose their best performances of the night and Kevin and Pam go for Sinead, Carrie picks Lemar and Sinead, while Richard plumps for Ainslie.

Malachi looks incredibly relieved when Cat announces that he's won the public vote with a 41% share. Nigel and Katie have to stand and wait for the student votes to be given. Nigel tells everyone not to worry as he's got his beautiful wife waiting for him, while Katie gives her familiar "Go with your hearts" speech. With three votes to his two, Katie is staying in the Academy. Nigel takes the news well and addresses the students, saying: "Keep it up guys. We're all creating a great show here. I love you all. Don't feel hard about your decision tonight. I'm going to have a beer and see my wife." A video message from his children is played and there's a few tears from the big man as he runs off stage and into the arms of his wife, who he lifts off the ground in a sweeping hug.

The teachers announce that David will be the first student on probation next week. He throws his arms in the air and whoops and says that he saw it coming. But his true feelings are revealed when he gets back to the Academy. Supping a beer, he leans back against the fireplace looking downtrodden while the students angrily express how unfair they thought it was. The furore prompts Richard to have a few words with David before bedtime. "Your chums obviously think it was a bit brutal," he says to David. "It was a double whammy for me tonight," the solemn Scot replies, "Nigel going was hard. The next week will be hard without him." David cheers up no end when the students round the night off with a water fight and he happily soaks a screaming Katie. After all, tomorrow is another day.

WEEK SIX

Interview
Nigel

FAMILY MAN NIGEL SAYS HE WAS READY TO LEAVE THE ACADEMY, BUT HE'S STILL PLANNING TO BECOME THE NEXT ROBBIE WILLIAMS, WHATEVER CARRIE SAYS.

How do you feel about being expelled?
It was the right time for me. It was six weeks away from my family and I really was ready to go. The thought of going back to the Academy that night was okay because it was a short week, but in my plea I said: "Listen guys don't worry, I've got a beautiful wife over there waiting for me." I was pleased to get votes from the two people I believe to be most talented, who are David and Lemar.

Who do you think will be next to go?
I truly hope it's Katie because I think she's the least talented. She is hugely talented, but out of the students that are in there, she's the least talented and I think on occasions she's been voted back in because she's the least threat. She could win it as well with the way pubic opinion is going. I have to say, I thought Ainslie's performance last week was the worst performance of the entire series and I couldn't believe it when the teachers said he was the best. I think he's a great performer and I think he'll go far, but I don't think he did great that night. I think there's a possibility he could leave as well and it would be a huge shock to him.

Do you think Katie will mind if she's expelled?
No, I don't think she will. I agree that she sees Fame Academy as a holiday and all she keeps saying is: "I've learnt so, so, so, so much!" I think she's made brilliant progress, but I still don't think she's as good as the others.

You didn't get on with Katie initially, so why did you vote for her instead of Pippa on the Live Showdown?
I prefer Katie's voice because I thought Pippa warbled. Pippa was also very private and when I'd try to talk to her she would kind of ignore me and it became apparent that she didn't like me. I didn't not vote for her because she didn't like me, but I honestly preferred Katie's voice. Plus, I thought about who I would prefer to spend another week with and that was Katie. Although I've heard Pippa's first single since I've been out – it's a dance version of Aerosmith's 'Don't Want To Miss a Thing' – and it's fantastic.

Do you regret any of the voting decisions you made?
Yes, I regret not voting for Marli. I made my decision based on friendships and how funny Malachi is and what a big TV maker he is inside the Academy; that was wrong. Malachi is a great guy and he's so funny, but he's never going to be a pop star. He's a folk singer, whereas Marli has a good chance of making it. I think people tactically voted her out because she's such a threat. She's so talented and once wrote a song for Liberty X. I don't know if it ever went on the album, but it shows you what she's capable of.

Do you think people are getting really serious about the voting now?
Yes, but why? You should be happy for the most talented person in the Academy to win. I knew I was never going to win.

How come?

Because it would have laughed in the face of everything the music industry stands for.

Do you think your age was a big deal in the Academy?

Yes. I think they thought they needed to put an older guy in, but they must have thought I was talented. I guess I was the most talented out of the older people.

Do you think being older made it hard for you to get on with some of the people in there?

To start with, yes. They stick together like kids at school and do giggly things in corners. Richard Park gave us a talk telling us that we were there to work and learn and it was clear that a lot of the girls in there thought it was just a riot. I really wanted to get down and work so I found that hard.

Carrie has said that you're not cut out to be the next Robbie Williams. How do you feel about that?

When Robbie Williams left Take That, I'm sure like everyone else Carrie thought he was the least likely to make it. So I think it's utter crap that anyone can judge what anyone is going to achieve. Everyone is entitled to their opinion, but you never know what people will do.

You and David got very close, didn't you?

Yes, I think David is amazing. People think he's a phoney because he smiles all the time, but he's not. That's just the way he is and he's a lovely bloke and so talented. He gave me such strength in the Academy.

You appear to be a big fan of Lemar as well?

I am, totally. I think he has the best voice in there, I just think he's incredible. He made me cry in the auditions when he sang 'Everything I Do'. I sat there and thought: "Why am I here?"

Tears were streaming down my face. He is unbelievably talented. He's learned to play the guitar while he's in there and he can write songs in his head. He's just amazing.

Who do you think is going to win Fame Academy?

I've said I want David to win, but I think Lemar will win. Sinead is a very hot contender and I think the more the teachers say that Lemar is going to win, the less chance he has of winning because the public will think he thinks he's something he's not.

You must have missed your family loads while you were away...

I missed my family tremendously. I'm a bit of a family man and I've never been apart from my kids for longer than a night. I was scared of getting in the helicopter after the first show as I knew that was it, there was no more contact. My mobile phone had been taken away and it all started to become real. The other guys were so excited because they didn't have a mortgage and a wife and dependants, but I was terrified. Until you have children no one can understand how much love you have for them. I can't express how much I love my children and it hurt because I was worried that people would think I was the worst dad in the world. I missed my children and my wife an unbelievable amount.

What else did you miss?

I missed my parents and my brothers and everyday things like walking the dogs and playing football and dropping my kids off at school. I missed taking my daughter horse

riding and sitting down and watching TV for ten minutes. You don't realise what you've got until it's taken away from you. That's why I was so miserable in the first week.

What do you make of the Malachi and Sinead situation?

I think it's been inflated a bit. I don't think Malachi really genuinely wants to have a relationship with Sinead on the outside. As for Sinead, I don't know. Malachi is a really good looking kid and Sinead is beautiful and they'd make an ideal pair, apart from the fact one is over six-foot and one is five foot two! I personally think it's for TV, but I also think there's some affection there. Only time will tell.

And what about Marli and Jeremy snogging?

Well they're both single, so they're both free to do what they want. But I don't think it's anything that's going to continue, I think it's just a bit of a laugh. Marli is very sexy and Jeremy is very handsome, so they'd make a great couple.

Have you been recognised a lot since you've left the Academy?

Yes, everywhere I go. In the hotel, in restaurants, walking around the shopping mall. I must have signed 700 autographs this week. I know I've been stereotyped as the housewives' favourite, but it's been a real mixture of people asking. I keep thinking: "This isn't happening." But it is.

What's next for you?

The Academy is a platform that you can launch yourself from and it's such a great opportunity to show people what you can achieve. I thank everyone for the support they've given me and I think if all I gain is a friendship with the guys in the Academy, that's enough for me because I know a lot of them are going far. I would be disappointed if I didn't make it as I've been singing since I was 16, but things are looking very encouraging and I would love to put an album together. Lionel Ritchie said to me that it's not always the Grade A students in life who get everything. He was never Grade A or Grade B when he was growing up and now look at him. And if I could be the next Lionel Ritchie... wow!

WE CHATTED TO PAM ONCE SHE'D SPENT SOME QUALITY TIME WITH THE BUDDING HIT-MAKERS TO FIND OUT WHO SHE THINKS ARE THE POTENTIAL WINNERS.

How is your Fame Academy experience going?

I'm loving being with the students. I've never been a teacher before and teaching songwriting is not an easy thing to do. It's a creative thing; it's like teaching painting to somebody who can't paint. It's a little different to the dancing and singing side, so it's been quite a challenge. It's something I'm enjoying because I'm learning a lot myself and I can see progress in the students already and I'm really excited about that.

How would you describe your role in Fame Academy?

I'm getting the students to think about different ways of writing. They're writing in groups, which a lot of them have never done before and I'm getting them to develop their own styles. Their personalities are starting to really come out, which is great. Some of the stuff they've had to do has been very difficult, but they're coping really well.

Who has surprised you with their songwriting abilities?

Pippa has never written before and a couple of the things she's done since have really surprised me. I was surprised by most of them though, to be honest. I didn't think they would be at the level they are. I think Ainslie and Marli have great songwriting abilities, they've both been songwriters before. Nigel is a good songwriter and Lemar has an amazing commercial ear and a great pop sensibility. His melodies are incredible; he's just got to open his mouth and it comes out. I don't know how

long he's been writing, but he's definitely got it. Camilla is also a great writer and hopefully she'll develop more. I would say Camilla and Lemar are the most commercial writers.

How weird was it watching Camilla perform 'Genie In a Bottle' when you wrote the song?

It was really hard for me to judge it because it probably looked a bit like sour grapes when I said anything negative. It was incredibly hard for Camilla because Christina Aguilera sang it originally and she has the most fantastic voice.

Do you think Camilla did a good job?

I thought she did really well. We spoke about her tuning and timing problems before she went on stage and she was aware she was doing it, but I don't think she locked into it all. I think her nerves got the better of her. Bless her heart, she did a great job, but she didn't quite get there. I haven't seen her since and I would very much like to tell her that I think she's got huge potential as an artist. She's a stunning looking girl and her voice is beautiful, but I think she needs to do a lot of work on it. I think she needs to strengthen her performance so the nerves don't get to her and that's going to take a few months. But she's definitely got something.

Who do you think has the best chance of winning?

If I'm going on talent and not tactics – because they're two different things – I would say either Ainslie, Lemar or Marli. I think those

three will last the longest. I pray they do. They've all got different things about them that are unique and I think that's what stands out the most. But I have to say, Sinead also shines for me.

Who do you think will go far because of the public and student votes?

Nigel could do well on the public vote, Katie could do well on the student vote, Malachi could do really well on the student vote because he's so loved and so adorable. It's so hard because I think any of the three I mentioned as winners could win or be tactically voted off at any time. So it's difficult to know who's going to win.

Who could go on to be the biggest star?

I think Ainslie is a superstar. He gets on stage and it's his. He wants it bad, you can see that. He's just so got that X factor and that rock star persona. He doesn't give a damn what anyone thinks about what he does, which is brilliant.

He's been quite rebellious so far hasn't he...

He has, but he listens in class. I was wondering how it would be for me – who the students probably view as a pop writer – coming in and asking them to write pop songs when pop isn't really their thing. I thought that I would get more grief, but they've worked really well with me, and I think they understand that I'm just trying to help them get started. I'm just helping them to hone their craft.

What's been the best moment in Fame Academy for you so far?

When Ainslie, Sinead and Malachi sang the song they'd written, 'Keep Me a Secret', it was the proudest moment of my life. I'd worked so hard to get that song on the show and get it to that point. I was absolutely bursting with pride and I'm so pleased that it was the first song that came out of the Academy. It's got a hit chorus and even Shania Twain said that it's going to be a big success. That's an amazing achievement because she's an amazing songwriter.

Is there anyone you've tried to push and have been disappointed with?

I'm a little disappointed with Katie. To be fair she hasn't written before, but she doesn't concentrate very hard in class, she's very scattered. I had to have a word with all of the students the other day and ask them to concentrate. There are a lot of time restrictions on them so it's important for them to concentrate at all times. Songwriters have days to write songs, but sometimes the students only have a matter of hours, so it is tough.

How hard do you find it choosing who is going to be on probation?

It's so tough. I dread Monday's, it's the worst thing. Especially when you know you're on camera and you know that they're going to see your comments. I absolutely hate it and I'm finding it more and more difficult as we go along.

How do you choose who to put on probation?

I would never put a student on probation for not being a good songwriter, but if they were disruptive in my class or they weren't on time or they were disrespectful, that would give me reason to put them on probation.

Ainslie is very talented, but he's been behaving pretty badly...

I brought this up one Grading Day because I wondered what people would think about the fact he'd been made A Grade when he'd been misbehaving. But his talent does shine through, thankfully.

Who do you think would embrace the pop star lifestyle and would love to win the prize most?

I think they'd all lap it up, actually. I would say Pippa, Lemar, Ainslie and Marli would love it most as far as the bright lights and the whole deal goes. I think Sinead and Malachi are probably more suited to being singer songwriters and the kind of artists that take a step back. David actually said to me the other day that he loves songwriting so much if he didn't make it as an artist he would be quite happy to take a back seat and write songs for other people, which I thought was great.

What do you think the Academy's oldest student, Nigel, will go on to do?

I adore Nigel and I think he's trying so hard in the Academy. It's probably been the toughest for him because he's got a wife and four kids waiting at home. Coming into the Academy and being the oldest person is tough because the music industry is very age-ist and very reluctant to sign anyone over the age of about 25, let alone over 30. I think he's going to find it tough, but I think he's got a great following of a certain age group. And he could probably have some

success making an album or two. He looks so good on stage, he really tears it up. He's a great performer.

And what about the youngest student, Katie?

I would love to see how Katie performed before because she totally crumbles when she gets on stage. I don't know whether that's something she's going to work on to get better at or whether she'll always be like that. I don't know if she's got it in her to overcome her fear of the stage. She's got a beautiful voice, but she needs to find a direction, as does Pippa.

Were you surprised to discover that David could songwrite?

Totally, I was blown away. We had a session to go through his songs and I was amazed. He certainly kept that quiet!

Finally, can you see any romances blossoming in the Academy?

I've seen David and Katie get on well, but I don't know if they're just friends. Camilla and Lemar definitely have a thing for each other and Marli and Ainslie do. Sinead and Malachi could happen, but I think Malachi is keener on Sinead then she is on Malachi. They all look good as couples, I have to say!

Monday

David is feeling a tad cheerier this morning after last night's probation blow. The teachers gather to discuss who will be joining him on probation, but the decision is getting tougher. Richard tells his colleagues that the Grade A student will be decided tomorrow. The students gather to watch the previous night's show. David was unhappy with his performance of 'Goodnight Girl' and as she predicted on Saturday, Katie was unhappy with her hair and felt "gross". Ainslie is concerned about his "bum notes scattered around the place" but Carrie is happy as larry with his offering and also enthuses over Malachi whom she says looked "absolutely stunning!" She also praises Lemar, but warns him about coping with his nerves.

The students are told that the third probationer – either Ainslie or Malachi – will be announced on Wednesday. The Headmaster also tells the students that he is not happy with the rule breaking which has been going on; in particular all the swearing and the previous night's water fight. He reveals that a party will be held on Wednesday night, but only if those responsible for the water fight own up within 24 hours. David goes to Richard's study to confess that he started the water fight and assures him that he doesn't need to look for anyone else in connection with the incident.

During a PDP session with Jeremy, the students admit their biggest regrets in the Academy. Whilst reading through the Yearbook they compiled in the first week, Ainslie admits:

The stress of probation gets too much for David and he leaves Kevin's dance class to sit on a sofa in the corridor. Kevin joins him and asks: "What are you most frustrated about?" "I felt so low last night when I went on stage," David replies tearfully, "as soon as they said they were going to announce it, I knew it was going to be me." There are almost tears from Katie too when she's told that she's the second student on probation this week. But her sadness turns to smiles when Richard tells her that as a reward for handling her six weeks' of probation so well, she'll be attending the premier of the new James Bond film 'Die Another Day' tonight in London's West End, so it's not all bad news after all.

"I think I most regret not getting to know people as much as I could have done." David says he wishes he could have talked to Naomi before he'd taken her place in the Academy, while Lemar said he regrets some of his student vote decisions. "I wish there was at least one vote for Marli, that moment felt a bit horrible," he says sadly.

Tuesday

After a tough morning's workout, Malachi relaxes by serenading Sinead with 'Have I Told You Lately That I Love You?' Katie admits to Jeremy that she really wants to win the Fame Academy prize now, especially after her brush with fame at the Bond premier last night. Carrie gathers the students together to

announce that Lionel Ritchie will be coming back to this week's Live Showdown to sing the song Lemar, Nigel and Camilla wrote to Lionel's melody. "Lemar's going to be doing the lead on the song because he's the only one left out of that original team, but you're all going to be singing on it," she informs the stunned group.

There's more news to come when she reveals that the students will be releasing an album of a selection of songs from the Live Showdow's in the second week of December. "You will leave this Academy as recording artists. Well done!" she grins.

The students perform the songs they've written about their fellow students. Katie has written one for Marli entitled 'Everything

to win. "I guess I have just had it in my head that I have been tootling along for a long time. It's just not feeling worthy, does that sound weird? It makes sense though doesn't it?" But Kevin isn't having any of it! "Well no it doesn't. You make it to the last few out of 36,000 applicants. I mean, are you talented or not?" Well said!

After a boozy evening, David and Katie have a pillow fight, with Katie claiming to be the winner! Katie and David's late night games are getting to be something of a habit...

Wednesday
Sinead finds it hard to get up and it takes a shouting Katie to rouse her. Katie tells Ainslie she is concerned about looking stupid when

"I FELT SO LOW LAST NIGHT WHEN I WENT ON STAGE, AS SOON AS THEY SAID THEY WERE GOING TO ANNOUNCE IT, I KNEW IT WAS GOING TO BE ME" DAVID

Changed', David has written one for Naomi, while Ainslie has written 'You're Beautiful' for Sinead.

"I had to write it, Sinead," Ainslie tells the blushing beauty. "You're one of those girls who's just beautiful and you have no idea. You're the only person who can't see it."

Sinead performs 'Sleep To Get Away', which she's written about Katie's probation drama, while Malachi sings 'Eyes So Blue' for – yep, you guessed it – Sinead. Finally Lemar sings 'Missing You' for ex-students Nigel and Camilla.

Kevin tells David, Lemar, Katie and Sinead that with a million pound prize up for grabs, they should start taking things more seriously. Malachi tells Kevin he doesn't feel he deserves

the students sing with Lionel Ritchie at the Live Showdown. Lemar is feeling under the weather again and sits out of Kevin's dance class to watch David leading the warm up. He is soon on hand to give Ainslie some advice in the gym and is thankfully feeling well enough to practice his dance routine for the Live Showdown that afternoon.

The teachers gather to discuss who will be joining Katie and David on probation. It's a choice between Ainslie and Malachi and the teachers just can't decide. After a heated discussion, they decide on Ainslie. The Headmaster delivers the news to the students and Ainslie looks devastated when his name is called out, while his fellow students try

DAVID **NO IDENTITY
COMING THROUGH
AT ALL**
CARRIE

KATIE **CLOSING THE
GAP, BUT THERE
ARE STILL OTHERS
AHEAD OF YOU**
RICHARD

AINSLIE **HAS A
TENDENCY NOT TO
SING AT HIS BEST
ON FRIDAY'S
SHOWDOWN'S**
RICHARD

ON PROBATION

to comfort him. Sitting on their bench outside Ainslie admits to Malachi: "Even though I thought it might happen, I hadn't prepared myself for it." Malachi has some pearls of wisdom for his friend, telling him: "Life's strange with its twists and its turns, as everyone of us sometimes learns."

Katie and Malachi give each other pedicures in the lounge and there's good news for Lemar when a doctor gives him the all clear. Richard announces that the students will be treated to a pub themed party tonight, with the dance studio boasting a waiter, snooker table, pub food and a pub quiz. The lucky winner of the quiz will receive a "Get out of dance class" voucher. The competition is on!

Malachi and Sinead hold hands in the lounge and after a telephone conversation with her boyfriend, Katie admits to Sinead that she loves him, but she isn't "in love" with him. The pub party kicks off and the students stock up on cocktails and scampi and chips and shoot some pool. David and Sinead are the very happy winners of the pub quiz and look lovingly at their coveted "Get out of dance class" vouchers!

Malachi, Ainslie and Katie go for a cigarette and have a heart to heart. Katie says she's missing Marli, while Malachi is concerned that he looks stupid chasing Sinead. Ainslie is worried he'll be expelled on Friday but Malachi tells his pal he's mad if he doesn't realise what a brilliant songwriter he is.

Thursday

The students prepare to head to Shepperton Studios for rehearsals, whilst nursing their hangovers. Ainslie is last to get on the bus to Shepperton and as he makes his way down the stairs he makes a plea to a nearby camera, saying: "Please let me stay one more week!"

Down at the studio the students excitedly pick up their fan mail and Ainslie is stunned to receive ten bouquets of flowers.

Back at the Academy, it's time for the students to make their farewell speeches. Katie kicks off by saying a simple: "Thanks for my time at the Academy… I love you all" David is next and tells his pals: "I'm a cheery, cheesy person and always will be. This could be my last day but

I'll support you all the way." Then it's Ainslie's turn to make his first ever probation speech. "I know I whinge and moan. I know I don't make friends easily. But at this stage I feel we are family!" he declares.

Jeremy holds a meeting with the students as he has a confession to make. "I want to tell you something that happened to me last week so that whatever you may or may not hear, at least you've heard it from me first and you've heard the truth," he begins, as the students look on a tad confused. "I was at a club, with lots of people, a bit of a BBC party. It was one of my nights out and Marli was there. We had a couple of drinks and we had a bit of a snog." It's open mouths and smiles a go-go and everyone looks stunned by his admission!

Ainslie is in a huggy mood and gives Katie a squeeze telling her that he doesn't know how she's handled being on probation six times. Then it's Malachi's turn for a bit of Ainslie hug love. Katie's rehearsals in the dance studio are interrupted by David sneaking in trussed up in a face mask and his pyjamas. Katie appears not to mind him dancing madly behind her while she's trying to concentrate, especially when he falls over and she gives him a "that'll teach you" look. Ah, those crazy kids!

Sing for Survival

IT'S 8PM AND AT SHEPPERTON STUDIOS, VANESSA AND DANAAN ARE RECORDING THEIR LINKS FOR BBC CHOICE AMONGST THE CHEERING CROWDS. THE MOSH-PIT IS PACKED TO THE RAFTERS AND THE FRIENDS AND FAMILY MEMBERS ARE MINGLING IN THEIR SEATING AREA. IN A NEW TWIST TO THE LIVE SHOWDOWN PROCEEDINGS, THE AUDIENCE MEMBERS WILL BE ABLE TO VOTE FOR WHOM THEY WANT TO STAY IN THE ACADEMY AND EVEN JONATHAN ROSS IS WATCHING THE SHOW FROM BESIDE THE TUTORS. WITH 30 MINUTES TO GO THE ATMOSPHERE IS ELECTRIC!

At 8.15pm the teaching faculty take their seats, aside from Carrie and Kevin who dart about, chatting to the students' parents and smiling at the banners, as well as boogie-ing and clapping along to the warm-up music. For the first time, the three probationers are filmed onstage for the introduction to the show, then they retire to the side of the stage to sip water, hug and generally try to keep their nerves in check. They wait patiently as Cat and Patrick run through their opening lines, with Patrick drawing particular

attention to Cat's mini-skirt, although she jokingly reassures the audience that they won't see anything they shouldn't: 'I'm wearing big pants!' she laughs.

Suddenly it's time for action and the first to perform his Survival Song is David, who works the room like a true professional with Elton John's 'Don't Let the Sun Go Down on Me'. Jumping for joy at the end of his two minutes, an ecstatic David beams as Carrie announces:'That was fantastic. He made it look effortless.'

Katie is next up and sets temperatures soaring with a sexy version of Kylie Minogue's 'Can't Get You Out of My Head'. Even though her microphone had to be changed with seconds to spare, Katie keeps her cool and Kevin acknowledges her composure by proudly raising his arms in support when she admits she thought she picked up well after a shaky start. Richard Park feels differently: 'OK. Not drop dead brilliant' he proclaims to gasps of surprise from the studio audience and an exasperated looking Jonathan Ross!

While Katie performs, Ainslie paces about near his marker and seems desperate to get his turn over and done with. After a brief introduction he bursts into action with an energetic rendition of The Pretenders 'Don't Get Me Wrong', complete with his trademark mad dancing, leaping around and even a rock star-esque throwing off of his self-customised suit jacket. Afterwards an excited Carrie shouts 'He sang flat, but who gives a 'bleep!' and Pam Sheyne confirms 'Whenever he performs a song, he makes it his own.'

The studio poll on the probationers is a close run thing, with Ainslie receiving 42% of the audience vote, David right behind him with 41% and Katie picking up 17%. Then it's on with the show as Lionel Ritchie comes onstage to play piano on his and the students' track ' Coming Back to You'. Lemar leads on vocals and Sinead chimes in for a duet before all the students stride onstage for the chorus. They are directed by a beaming Mr Ritchie, who thinks all the students have made a 'big step forward, a big leap' since he last came on the show and he proudly hugs Lemar and Malachi as they lead the group offstage.

It's time for some more show-stopping numbers as Lemar breezes through the funky choreography of his song, Stevie Wonder's soulful 'Don't You Worry 'Bout a Thing'. Jeremy decides it was an awesome performance, but once more Richard is reserved in his praise, commenting 'A difficult song, he did his best'. Even Kevin is soon fighting to be heard over the audience reaction when he gives Sinead some stern criticism over her spontaneous sashay down to the centre podium during her version of 'Ironic' by Alanis Morrisette. 'She commanded the stage, but she should have stayed in the lighting at the back. 'Boo' as much as you like, she shouldn't have moved!'

Finally, Malachi gets to saunter down the little-used raised catwalk and staircase when he sings Joe Cocker's 'Have I Told You Lately', continuing right through the crowds and smiling as he spots good luck banners from his fans. An admiring Jeremy calls him 'Magic Malachi' and Kevin agrees it

was a 'confident, strong performance.' Sadly, the luck of the Irish isn't with the magical man tonight and he is announced as the first of this week's probationers at the end of the show, much to his Dad's disgust!

All too quickly, Cat and Patrick reveal the winner of the public vote and with 42% of the 1 million viewer calls made tonight, David keeps his place in the Academy. Cat gets swung in the air and tells the exuberant Scot to 'get down, Health and Safety will kill us!' when he stands on his seat to soak up the rapturous audience applause. It's left to our winner to cast the final student vote and he joins Malachi, Sinead and Lemar in unanimously voting to save Ainslie. It's an emotional moment as Katie watches her Academy Report and is comforted by the students, the floor manager ,the technicians and Patrick, while Ainslie admits to Cat: 'I thought it was a bit of a shambles tonight, but thanks!'

Katie's final words to her fellow students before she runs down to her family and boyfriend are 'I love you so much, thanks for making this so special. You're the best' and then the six-times probationer leaves the studio on a wave of cheers. Keep your chin up, Katie, you're a star!

Interview
Katie

PROBATION PRINCESS KATIE JUST KEPT ON BOUNCING BACK, BUT ACADEMY LIFE WASN'T ALWAYS EASY FOR HER. HERE SHE REVEALS ALL ABOUT KEVIN, CONFIDENCE AND HER PROBLEMS WITH CARRIE.

How are you feeling now you're out of the Academy?
It's all really good and exciting. I'm missing everybody loads and I'm really missing the singing lessons and stuff. I learnt so much.

Did you expect to go this week?
When I first started going on probation I was like: "Oh I'm gonna go, I'm gonna go." So I expected to go every week. But after a while I stopped thinking about it. I lived out of my suitcase – I never unpacked – but I tried not to have any expectations. I'd just go with the flow.

Was it stressful being on probation all the time?
Yeah, it was really hard. But I think it made me strong and built up my confidence and it was really good getting to sing solo every week.

Can you see a change in yourself from when you first went in?
Definitely, I've got so much more confidence on stage. I'd only sung one style before and I'd never had to perform in that way before. Then all of a sudden I'm in front of all these people and it was like "Aaaargghhhhh!" I was so scared, but as the weeks went on I got more confident and it got easier.

Were you really aware of the cameras?
For the first week or two I worried what I said all the time. But after that I completely forgot they were there and I was just myself. But then when I went to bed I'd be like: "Why did I say that? Why did I do that? People saw me!" And I would panic about everything.

What was the most nerve-racking thing about performing?
You know that everybody you know is watching it and criticising. I used to sit at home watching TV going: "Oh look at the way she did that, she didn't do that right." But when you have to get up and do it, it just doesn't happen how you expect. You know what you've got to do, but the pressure is on and things don't come out right.

What do you really wish people hadn't seen?
When I got drunk and was talking about Kevin. It's so embarrassing. I haven't seen it, but everyone keeps telling me about it.

Yes, you were very, erm, descriptive about what you would like to do with Kevin...
I know. It's the most embarrassing thing I've ever done. The thing is, I could hardly remember it the next day. I got drunk another time and told Kevin I was in love with him and I didn't remember that either, so I went to his lesson and didn't think anything of it. Then everybody reminded me and it all came flooding back.

Did your mum see all the saucy things you said about Kevin?
I think so, but she hasn't said anything!

How are you feeling about Kevin now?
It's not like I'm madly head over heels in love with him or anything. It was just because I was stuck in the Academy. It's so funny because he never really mentioned it to me or anything.

Some people thought that you and David might get together...
I know. I think it's just because I'm quite a flirty person, but I didn't fancy him.

What do you make of the Malachi and Sinead situation?
I think it's just a bit of a joke and they're just playing it up now. If there really is anything in it they probably won't do anything while they're in the Academy. They'll wait until they've come out. I think if it was up to Malachi something would happen, but I'm not sure if Sinead feels the same way.

What do you think of Ainslie's bizarre habit of talking to himself?
It's really weird because I never realised he did that. People have been telling me stuff that he's done and I'm like: "Ainslie, what are you doing?" He's a bit weird anyway, but not in a bad way. That's just Ainslie. It's his way of coping with all the stress of everything that's going on.

Who were you closest to in the Academy?
Marli. And I also got on really well with David and Malachi.

Everyone seems to love Malachi...
He's brilliant. He's really funny, but he's got this really sensitive side and he's always there for you.

Do you regret not voting for Marli the night she was expelled?
That was the most difficult thing I've ever had to do. I don't really know what made me choose Malachi. When she didn't get any votes I felt so bad. We'd been saying how awful it would be if nobody voted for you and she was probably my best friend in the Academy I felt awful. I didn't know what to do because there were so many reasons I wanted each of them to stay.

What was the deciding factor?
I thought that Malachi needed a bit more help, whereas Marli could go out there and make it. Marli hasn't really changed since she's been in the Academy. She hasn't progressed that much because she's a star anyway and she's got everything she needs – her image, her voice, her looks, her confidence – everything. But there's more for Malachi to work on. And because I saw it as more of a learning experience, I kept Malachi in. I thought the longer he stays in the more he can improve and the more chance he'll have of making it when he gets out. But then Marli should have had the chance to win the prize because she's so good. It's so hard. You try to do the right thing, but there is no right thing.

Who do you think will go out this week out of Ainslie, Malachi and Sinead?
I think it will be whoever is best on the night. When I was voting I tried not to vote on the friendship side, I tried to vote on what was right.

Who do you think will win?
Any of the students who are left could. They're all so talented in different ways. I know they're all capable of winning.

What was your favourite moment in the Academy?
Meeting Lionel Ritchie. It was amazing, so brilliant. It was such an experience. I just wanted to scream, but of course I couldn't! It was really good meeting Mariah as well. I thought she was going to be a diva, but she wasn't actually that bad. She was really friendly.

You had some problems with Carrie in the Academy, didn't you?
Yes. I think it was my fifth week on probation and we were all having a moan. You're in such a weird environment and people put things into your head, so you can get paranoid. Because of some of the comments that Carrie had made I started saying I hated her and stuff. Then when they said I was going to the Bond premiere with her I was like: "Noooooo!" So I told her everything and she was fine about it. She had been a bit off with me as well so it cleared the air. I got on fine with all the other teachers, though.

What was the most upsetting comment you got from the teachers?
That I was the worst student. They all told me they were wrong and stuff, but they never said it on TV. It's one thing saying it and then taking it back, but no-one else knew that they'd taken it back after they had said it on national television. That really got me down.

What was your worst moment in the Academy overall?
On the Live Showdowns right in the beginning because I sang so out of tune because I was so nervous. It was so frustrating because I knew there was so much in me and there still is.

It was awful that people were seeing me singing like that. I thought: "Should I just leave? Can I do this?" I thought it was going to be the end of my career before I'd even started. But as the weeks went on things started coming together.

Which of the students do you think you'll stay in touch with?
Marli, mostly. I've spoken to her a couple of times on the phone and we're meeting up soon. But I'd like to stay in touch with all of them.

Have you been recognised a lot since you've been out?
Yes, it's so weird! I was in a shop the other day and all these screaming girls came in and asked for my autograph and wanted to hug me. It was brilliant.

What's next for you?
I haven't really got a plan. It's exciting because I don't really know where I'm going or what I'm doing. I'll just see where I end up. But I definitely want to keep on singing.

Interview
Jeremy

EVEN THOUGH JEREMY HAD ONLY BEEN IN THE ACADEMY FOR A FEW WEEKS WHEN WE GRABBED HIM FOR A CHAT, THE FEMALE STUDENTS' FLIRTING WAS ALREADY GETTING A BIT MUCH FOR HIM!

How are you enjoying Fame Academy?
It's great, I'm really enjoying it. It's pretty busy as I have to be around whenever the students need me and I often have to stay up until they decide to stop messing about and go to bed.

You're pretty close to the students, so do you ever get nervous during the student vote?
Totally. I know all of the students pretty well and I don't want any of them to go. It's so hard for the students having to make that decision. A lot of them feel really bad afterwards. It's tough.

How do you see your role in Fame Academy?
I'm the shoulder to cry on. I'm someone who they can talk to and know that what they say won't be used against them in their grading, because I don't have anything to do with that. I'm also here to keep morale going and address any group issues that people may feel uncomfortable with. The issues tend to come up on Friday nights, because sometimes when we get back to the Academy the students are furious about how things have gone and the comments which have been made by the teachers. Primarily I'm here so the students can have a moan about who's getting on their nerves, or if they're upset about being on probation. Anything, really.

And of course, there are the PDP sessions...
Yes, they're related to the wider experience of when the students leave the Academy and how they're going to be viewed by the press and public. But they can be about anything. The other night we did something about how to interpret the lyrics of songs because the students were singing stuff but not really knowing what they were singing about or why.

Which has been your favourite PDP session?
The students all enjoyed the one with the song lyrics because it gave them an insight into why a lyric was written. It was an opportunity for them to be creative, have some fun, and let off some energy. Everything we do in the Academy is geared towards the Live Showdown, so they need a chance to let off some steam somehow and the PDP sessions are perfect for that. We did a great game called Stroke My Ego the other night, which they all got a great boost from. They'd all been feeling a bit down and I think they felt better about themselves afterwards.

Which student do you think is missing home most?
Nigel, because he's a married man with children. But Pippa is probably missing it even more than Nigel. She's really close to her family and her mum is like a rock for her. She's also really close to her boyfriend. Malachi is also missing home. He's very worried about how he's being perceived by his parents and is worried that he's letting them down because of some of his antics.

Now, you appear to flirt with the girls in the Academy rather a lot...
Of course I do, absolutely! I have a toolbox of skills that I can dip into to get what I think is necessary or best for the students. And if flirting with the girls or being laddish with the guys helps a bit, then certainly I'll do it. But it's

not as bad as the way the girls flirt with me, I have to say. It's full on. I have to walk out sometimes because it gets too much!

How did you cope when Marli said she was thinking of walking out?

I don't know if Marli was doing that to get her own way or not, but at the end of the day, it's the students' choice. In the grand scheme of things, if she had walked out it would have been a mistake because the weeks the students spend in the Academy are a drop in the ocean compared to the lifetime they could spend in the music industry. If someone decides they really to want to leave then I'll open the door and close it behind them, but I don't think anyone is seriously going to do that.

Was it hard having to comfort Naomi when she had to leave?

Nobody wanted Naomi to go, so it was hard. But on the other hand, it was made easier by the fact that she and everyone knew that it was in her best interests. She couldn't stay because it would have been a dangerous gamble. She could have done permanent damage to her voice.

Why do you think Ainslie is being so rebellious?

I just think he kicked against some the rules a little bit. He wasn't happy about being "institutionalised" and being told what to do and when. He's said to me that he feels really caged in and can't express himself. He questions all the rules and has the attitude that if we want him to follow them, he wants to know why and how it will benefit him or the group, which is fair enough. I think he also likes to flirt with the wild side a little bit and find out what it's like to be a bit rock'n'roll. Also, he knows he's being watched 24 hours a day, so maybe he's showing the public that he fits into the pop star role?

Do you think there will be any romances?

I think that if Lemar wasn't the kind of bloke he is, something would have kicked off between him and Camilla by now. It still may at a future date. But he knows that his family and girlfriend are watching him and he's got morals that he's going to stick by. I think Malachi would like a romance with anybody who will have him, including the statues in the lounge that he tries to chat up. There seems to be something between David and Katie and for a while I thought Naomi and Ainslie might get together. Then again, I did think maybe Ainslie and Marli might get together as well.

Who do you think would be most suited to the pop star lifestyle the Fame Academy prize offers?

I think Ainslie thinks he would be and he's already flirting with the pop star lifestyle in the Academy. But he's had a few wake-up calls and he's got to realise that he's a small fish in a big pond. I think Sinead would deal with it really well because she's very grounded. She's not blown away by all the glam and glitz. I think Lemar would deal with it very well too. He keeps himself a bit separate from the group and commands his own space. He's got his religion, which is very important to him – but he doesn't make a big fuss of it – and I think that keeps him very level headed. He's also very, very talented. Although he keeps himself a bit distant from people, they've got a huge amount of respect for him, as they have for Sinead.

Who do you think is going to win Fame Academy?

I keep changing my mind. Initially I thought it was going to be Ainslie or Marli, but I'm not so sure now. When everyone came in, Ainslie and Marli were quite far ahead of the pack, but people are working hard in their classes and they're rapidly catching up. Look at how Sinead and Lemar have come on; they're fantastic. They've got to be considered potential winners of this competition.

week Eight

AINSLIE **NEEDS TO GIVE A SMALLER PERFORMANCE VISUALLY AS WELL AS VOCALLY**
CARRIE

GREAT PERFORMER BUT NEEDS TO WORK ON HIS TUNING
KEVIN

AINSLIE IS DESPERATELY TRYING TO FIND HIMSELF
RICHARD

ON PROBATION

Saturday

Following some after-show blues yesterday evening, the five remaining students are still a bit out of sorts. David tells Sinead that he's glad he won the public vote as he's unimpressed that Ainslie gets away with singing off-key, Malachi is missing Katie and Ainslie is disturbed by David's piano playing while he is working on some songs and has a tantrum. Even the usually calm Sinead argues with Richard Park over his comments on Lemar's performance during the Showdown post-mortem. The Headmaster eventually pulls rank, silencing the group decisively: "I'm being spoken to as if I've missed something. I haven't."

Lemar enjoys his outing to 'The Saturday Show', especially as he gets to sign autographs! Celtic lads David and Malachi are given a spray-on fake-tan treatment and flirty Malachi declares it "the best sensation I've had since I've been in this place!"

An acoustic session results in Jeremy and Pam each singing their own songs to the students and later Jeremy does his best to cheer up a despondent Malachi with his impersonations of Katie and Ainslie. Unfortunately, a subsequent PDP session deflates the Irishman even more when each student is given an insight into the public's opinion of them from messages posted on the website. David, Sinead and Lemar all scoff at their criticisms, which includes respectively "cheesy", "turns on the charm for the boys" and "doesn't try hard enough". Ainslie demands to hear the "really dark, nasty, intense ones" but Malachi is left depressed by an accusation that he is "sleazy". He sums up his mood by solemnly telling Jeremy "I think I could've had a better day for that PDP session." Roll on tomorrow for everyone, then...

Sunday

Ainslie and Malachi are back on form and dress up in 'Kids from Fame' style headbands for Kevin's workout. David and Sinead think they've got a lie-in after securing 'get-out-of-class-free' tickets for winning Jeremy's pub quiz game, except the tickets have gone missing. David accuses all and sundry of thievery as he and Sinead reluctantly attend the boxing class. Sinead has a tearful run-in with Kevin over her ad-lib moves on Friday night: "I had to do it because the vocals were so bad" she reasons. Kevin reiterates the hard work that goes into setting up the stage lighting but Sinead storms off, recovering later when Kevin reassures her "If you want to go wild, then tell me and we can do it."

Carrie asks each person to write a third-person critique of Friday's performances. Sinead reviews herself with "her attempt (at vocal control) made me cringe", Ainslie decides his "concept of tune and melody have been abandoned" and Malachi states "with the competition left, he needs to improve". David is more confident "having upped a gear" and Lemar teases he may not be the new Marvin Gaye, but "He may be a new something – we'll have to wait and see."

A sixties music theme is announced for this week and Ainslie threatens to walk out in protest! To compensate, David, Malachi and Ainslie get tipsy and play pranks around the Academy, including making fake emergency calls on the internal hotline and having a drunken heart to heart on probation blues.

Monday

After Kevin hauled a rowdy David and Malachi back into the Academy last night, the boys also have storming hangovers to deal with. David is saved from choreography class by his free pass mysteriously turning up in Malachi's pocket, so it's back to bed for him and a leisurely breakfast for Sinead. All the students are feeling generally exhausted, homesick, run-down and missing the outside world. Sinead is announced as the second probationer to Sing for Survival due to her lack of dedication to the rehearsal process.

Kevin, Pam and Carrie are all sure it's the right thing to do, with Kevin confirming "Sinead has made the decision for us." However, the third probationer will not be announced until further discussions on Wednesday. Demoralised David is confronted by Carrie over his frustration at never being the tutor's favourite performer at the Showdown. Carrie firmly tells him "I know it's hard for you, but now is not the time to get bitter." Whilst Malachi continues to be Mr Doom and Gloom when he confides in Ainslie "I've got a feeling that I'm going to be going home, so I have." Jeremy gets a frosty reception from the worn-out group when he asks them to grade themselves from best to worst in categories such as 'best vocalist', 'most likely sex symbol' and 'most likely to break the rules'. David sums up the mood of the gang by declaring "I don't like these games." Oh dear.

Tuesday

Kevin decides to have a go at this PDP lark to cheer the students up, but it rapidly descends into a "let's-tickle-Ainslie" session. Spirits are lifted when Richard announces that the group will all perform Lemar and Ainslie's song, 'Lullaby' on Friday. Things get even better for Ainslie when he and Malachi are given 'Bad Bad Butcher' t-shirts that a fan has made for them (Well done, Mr John Wright!). A tribute rendition of the ditty is duly performed.

Ainslie discusses with Jeremy how much he wants to stay in the Academy: "I don't want to watch the last week from my living room." There's a harsh reality check in store tonight however, when Steve Lilywhite, MD of Mercury Records and producer of artists such as the Rolling Stones, U2 and Darius, pays a late-night visit to the Academy. His message to everyone is "There's a big difference between winning and coming second or third." Specific comments are directed at Ainslie about not becoming complacent, David should "concentrate more" and Steve feels that Sinead isn't "taking enough

advantage of being the last girl." David defends himself and afterwards describes his session as "a big kick in the face" whilst Ainslie feels it was a "freak you out and kick your arse meeting". Something must have struck a nerve in each student however, as Ainslie decides to quit smoking and everyone else goes off to practice their Showdown songs before bed.

Wednesday

Sinead is up and at 'em today and for the first time since entering the Academy, rehearses her Survival song before breakfast. Ainslie lies in bed pondering his decision to stop smoking and is resolute until after lunch, when it is announced that he will be the third student on probation. He listens to Richard's words quietly, but afterwards is determined to make himself heard and tackles the Headteacher in his office about his comments. "I just resent the way there's a load of rubbish thrown in your face. If only you just said 'There were a few bum notes' …instead it feels there's a list of things that I'm not sure exist." Richard takes his time with his reply, assuring Ainslie "I know exactly where you're coming from. I know what you can do. The chances are there." Carrie tells the students that the three probationers will be singing a trio on Friday night and they immediately start to work on Sonny and Cher's classic 'I Got You Babe'. It all gets a bit much for Ainslie and after their session he has a cry on Jo's shoulder to unbottle some of his tension. A phone call with his dad helps to cheer him up though.

BBC Choice are rewarding the hardworking group with a night on the tiles but there's a catch. They have to compete with a live one minute version of Frank Sinatra's 'My Way'. With cabin-fever at an all time high, everyone leaps at the opportunity for some time out of the Academy. The three students with the highest number of votes will get taken to the Jazz Café in North West London. An afternoon of fervent rehearsal beckons and Vanessa and Danaan film

SINEAD **SHE IS FINDING IT DIFFICULT TO WRITE IN HERE. SHE HAS TO DELIVER** PAM

ON PROBATION DUE TO HER FRIDAY NIGHT PERFORMANCE CARRIE

DOESN'T REHEARSE AS MUCH AS SHE SHOULD DO RICHARD

MALACHI **NEEDS TO PULL OFF A NERVE-FREE PERFORMANCE** CARRIE

HASN'T DEVELOPED OUT OF BEING A SINGER OF GREAT IRISH-TYPE FOLK SONGS RICHARD

ON PROBATION

LEMAR

LEMAR SPENDS
TOO MUCH TIME
SLEEPING. HIS
VOICE ISN'T
WARMED UP AND
WE DON'T SEE HIS
PERSONALITY IF
HE'S ASLEEP

CARRIE

DAVID

MY HARDEST
WORKING STUDENT

PAM

HE'S FOUND A
FULLER VOICE
AND A BIGGER
SOUND. HE'S
GONE FROM BEING
A BOY TO A MAN

CARRIE

TUTOR
COMMENTS

the show next door to the lounge area, where the students are watching the TV broadcast. An astonishing 35,000 votes are cast in five minutes and it's David, Lemar and Sinead who get whisked off in the waiting limo. Malachi and Ainslie can't hide their disappointment at being left behind, but Carrie and Kevin take pity on them and they all spend the evening drinking wine and chatting, laughing at Ainslie's toast of "Here's to being the least popular people in the Academy!" The foursome talk openly about their Academy experiences, with the tutors answering the boys queries about how much the students' own comments affect them. "We accept that it's part of the job" Carrie states. "I don't accept it. It really irritates me" responds Kevin, prompting the lads to beat a hasty retreat. The dance tutor does show his softer side once they are out of the room, by confessing "I definitely would have smashed something by now. I love these guys."

Thursday

David is amazed at how well-received the students were last night on their outing: "I was talking to people and they all said that the five that are still in here will be huge when they come out". Malachi is more cautious about this sentiment, quoting Carrie who has told him they could be "riding on fame for a couple of months and then it will be someone else's turn." Malachi serenades a flustered Carrie with his rendition of 'Something' by The Beatles, dropping down on one knee, much to Kevin's amusement. Sinead's throat is causing her trouble, but a doctor's visit reassures everyone that it's nothing serious, just a minor throat infection. Sinead later admits in a webchat that while sharing a room with Malachi and Ainslie is "alright" she would much rather have Pippa back in the Academy as she was "a really bubbly girl, very genuine." Kevin is proud of David's stage choreography this week, telling the other tutors "he's getting up there and commanding the stage" and Carrie agrees, teasing them with "David wants to give Ainslie a run for his money – I say bring it on!" Finally, Lemar seems to be overcoming the criticism of his breathing technique and has made good progress with his version of 'Yesterday'.

Speech time arrives and Malachi is more reflective than usual, declaring "I find myself up

against two great friends for a place in the Academy. Thanks for being such lovely people." Sinead ends her first ever probation speech on a positive note: "We need to pick ourselves up and really go for it." Finally, Ainslie says his piece: "I've come to realise how much progress you can make as a performer and a person. If you hear a bum note, crucify me for it."

The evening ends as so many have before, with Ainslie and Malachi having a chat on their favourite bench on the terrace, reminiscing about the good times and having a hug to celebrate how well they've done so far. Never being ones to stay downhearted for long, they round off their evening by joining David in the dance studio and jumping around as he rehearses Stevie Wonder's 'For Once in My Life'. One thing's for sure, whoever leaves this Friday, the Academy is going to get a lot quieter.

Friday

Before hitting the now familiar road to Shepperton Studios, Sinead admits that she hasn't made up her mind who she will vote for if she wins the public vote this evening and has to choose between Ainslie and Malachi. "I'd just have to wait and see how they'd performed" she states fairly. A tough choice could well beckon soon, but a lot can happen in the course of one evening...

Rehearsal Day

IT'S FRIDAY AFTERNOON, WHICH MEANS IT'S
REHEARSAL TIME FOR THE STUDENTS OF
FAME ACADEMY.

They've all travelled by coach to Shepperton Studios where they're about to practice for tonight's Live Showdown, as well as getting their hair, make up and outfits sorted. Putting such a huge show together each week is a big deal and everything must be perfect. So it's practice, practice, practice. The probationers have already run through their songs several times and are pulling out all the stops in the hope that they will win the public vote tonight.

The Fame Academy studio looks much bigger without the audience to fill it and despite it being freezing outside, it's warm in the warehouse style space, where there is tea and coffee on tap. Carrie, Jo, Pam and Kevin are watching the rehearsals from the sidelines in their civvies, giving advice when it's needed. Kevin looks every inch the pop star himself in huge shades and baggy jeans, while Carrie is wrapped up in her warm parka.

Sinead, Malachi and Ainslie are rehearsing their version of 'Stand By Me', with Carrie giving Ainslie some pointers about pitching. Jo accompanies them on piano and when they finish, Lemar plants a kiss on her cheek as she walks past him. Ainslie carries on practising the song while the stage is set up for the next track. All five remaining students take up their positions on stage and gear up to practice a special song (all will be revealed in the Live Showdown). While they're waiting, Malachi breaks into 'You Ain't Nothing But a Hound Dog'. Ainslie also decides to have a singsong, leading his friends in a chorus of: "We are the kids from fame, we have no shame!" Meanwhile, David comes over a bit Billy Joel and plays 'Uptown Girl' on the piano, and Sinead sings George Harrison's 'While My Guitar Gently Weeps'.

It's time to practice the group song, which they run through five times. They regularly consult Jo and Carrie throughout to make sure they're hitting the notes properly, while Kevin shouts the odd instruction about their positioning.

All of the students and teachers except for Lemar, David and Kevin take a tea break. Lemar has to practice his solo and David has stayed behind to watch him. Before he takes to the stage Lemar has a swig of water from a black plastic bottle that boasts a sticker with his name on it. All the students have them nestling by their feet under their seats at the side of the stage in case they get dehydrated under the scorching studio lights. Lemar breaks into song, singing: "Yesterday, all my troubles were so far away." Kevin looks around worriedly for Carrie realising that he's sung "were" instead of "seemed", but the flame haired teacher is nowhere to be found. Afterwards Kevin corrects him and Lemar lets out a long "Aarrghhhh" of despair.

David is next to practice his solo and he comes on stage doing a natty dance routine and breaks into 'For Once In My Life'. He gets a whoop from the watching crew and obviously feeling encouraged, gets down on his knees and sings to an imaginary audience in the mosh pit. When he's finished he and Kevin do a high five before Kevin takes him through some of the moves. He runs through the song again and Kevin gives him a round of applause before joining him on stage for a quick congratulatory boogie around. It seems that Kevin is pleased as punch with David's dancing progress. Let's just hope he can pull if off during the real show later!

Sing for Survival

IT'S FRIDAY NIGHT AND THAT CAN ONLY MEAN ONE THING — ANOTHER ALL-SINGING, ALL-DANCING LIVE SHOWDOWN! THE AUDIENCE ARE POURING INTO THE FAME ACADEMY STUDIO DOWN AT SHEPPERTON AND THE ATMOSPHERE IS MORE TENSE THAN EVER BEFORE. THERE ARE ONLY FIVE STUDENTS LEFT AND ONE WILL WAVE GOODBYE TO THE PRIZE OF A LIFETIME TONIGHT.

Once the BBC Choice links have been recorded and the warm up guy has done a banner check to make sure that none of them feature swear words or are in the way of the cameras, everyone takes their positions. Tutors Pam, Carrie, Kevin and Jeremy enter the studio to a mixture of cheers and boos from the audience, while poor Richard gets mainly pantomime villain style boos.

Sinead, Malachi and Ainslie take their places on the stage. The audience go absolutely wild as the probationers wave and Sinead tilts her cerise hat in their direction. The trio have a massive hug, then David and Lemar enter from the backstage door. The audience response is extraordinary, with girls screaming out Lemar's name. The three probationers look fairly calm and collected, apart from Ainslie who can't keep still. One of the stylists runs onto the stage and gives Sinead a quick brush down and a reassuring smile and then the show kicks off. Cat looks

stunning in a slinky black dress and gold heels and
Patrick escorts her up the runway dressed in his
trademark suit, T-shirt and trainers to the biggest
round of applause yet.

Malachi is the first of the probationers to sing
and Cat gives him a hug and a kiss after he tells
her: "Whoever wins, I'll be happy for them." His
Survival Song is 'Something' by The Beatles and
Richard has a huge grin on his face throughout
his performance. Afterwards Carrie gushes: "He
really brought that off tonight." When Patrick
asks Pam which of the probationers will be
missed most if they go tonight, her reply is
"Malachi, without a doubt. He can turn the mood
of the Academy in a sentence." Malachi himself
takes the chance to tease Jeremy for: "messing
around outside the Academy," referring to his
recently exposed dalliance with Marli. Very cheeky!

Ainslie is pacing back and forth on stage and doing
odd monkey-like movements in preparation for his

performance. "I think for once I might sing in tune!" he jokes to Cat, before launching into
The Kinks raunchy 'You Really Got Me Going'. He puts on the show of his life, writhing
around the floor and rocking with the microphone stand. Once his song is over he walks
to the side of the stage to let the audience grab his legs and then stage dives on top of
them, eventually falling on to the floor. The teachers – who are in the middle of being
interviewed by Patrick – turn round when they hear the thud and catch Ainslie
climbing back onto the stage with a grin on his face.

Carrie says that Ainslie is "the kind of artist you either love or hate, but he's
not the kind of person to compromise," then gives him a thumbs-up. Ainslie is
thrilled, and Cat declares: "I don't think we've ever had quite so much thrusting
on the BBC!"

Sinead is the final probationer to perform and she has plenty of support in
the shape of her sister and uncle who have flown in from New York specially to
see her. "Thank you so much. We're gonna party!" she shouts. Sinead's take on
Dionne Warwick's 'Walk On By' is so smooth that Carrie admits no-one would have
noticed she made a lyrical mistake in repeating the same verse twice. "They will
now. She'll thank you for that!" Patrick laughs as the audience boo the vocal
coach for pointing out the slip-up.

Lemar is next to sing and does his classy rendition of 'Yesterday'. His Dad
sings along and looks amazingly proud. When he finishes, Lemar smiles and
blows kisses to the adoring audience, including a special one to his parents.
Carrie is impressed: "That was an amazing show stopping performance."
But Richard isn't convinced: "There's room for growth. I find that slightly
uninspiring." For that he earns himself the biggest boo of the evening so far.

The audience cast their own votes and while the results come through there's time for Patrick to talk to the probationers supporters. Sinead's sister admits that the good people of New York love the Irish songstress and Sinead looks especially pleased to hear that she has a big following amongst the police department and fire fighters! Ainslie's girlfriend Bernadette says that Ainslie: "always gives an outstanding performance," while Malachi's sister says that the Academy joker has: "got the charm, looks, personality, and he's certainly got the talent." The results are in and Ainslie is the audience's clear favourite with 42% of the votes. Sinead is second with 32%, and Malachi comes in third with 26%.

David is the final student to sing solo and there's plenty of eyebrow raising, smiling and dancing as he belts out 'For Once In My Life'. But he doesn't win Carrie's vote. "He shouldn't try to compete with Ainslie," she says. Kevin agrees. "I would never compare the two. He cannot out-perform the Academy performance King." David looks dejected, whilst Ainslie is clearly not happy about the teacher's comments and pointedly gives David a supportive hug.

The probationers sing together for the last time and it's a lovely version of 'Stand By Me' with Jo's piano accompaniment. Then it's time for all the remaining students to sing together and they perform Lemar and Ainslie's self-penned song, 'Lullaby'. Afterwards Pam is slightly overcome. "I'm so proud!" she says, before revealing that the track has made it onto the Fame Academy album.

Patrick asks the teachers who shone for them and Kevin, Pam and Carrie all choose Ainslie, while Richard goes for the probationers' version of 'Stand By Me'.

It's results time and the students take their places centre stage. Cat announces that over a million phone votes have been cast and Sinead is the lucky winner with 38% of them. She looks amazed but also incredibly unhappy about the prospect of having to vote for either Ainslie or Malachi. There are only three votes to be counted up this week and having won two of them from David and Lemar, Ainslie is heading back to the Academy while Malachi must go on his merry way. Ainslie and Malachi hug, then Malachi kisses Sinead and thanks her for voting for him. Ainslie tells everyone: "This isn't the way I wanted to be going back... It'll be a completely different place without Malachi." The big Irishman is still his usual cheery self and gives the teachers a clap, waves to his fellow students, then runs down the runway and into his mum's arms, grabbing the audiences' hands as he does so.

But the night is not over yet; the teachers have still to announce who will be on probation next week. None of the students are that shocked to discover that they will all Sing For Survival during next week's show and David admits he's pretty pleased about the news. "I thought it was going to be me, so I'm quite relieved!" he laughs. But will he be laughing next week? We'll have to wait and see...

After the show the four remaining students are ushered into in the swanky Fame Academy bus, which boasts pop star-esque blacked out windows. Some of the friends and family wandering past spot them and start shouting to get their attention. They're soon asked to move on by the production team, but are reluctant to leave their loved ones. The students manage to sneak to the door of the bus and give waves and air kisses before being called back inside.

Never one to miss an opportunity, one of the crew on board the bus asks the assembled crowd if anyone could spare a cigarette for Ainslie. So much for having given up!

Interview
Malachi

WE CAUGHT UP WITH THE IRISH UBER-CHARMER AND ALL ROUND TOP BLOKE TO GET THE GOSSIP ON HIM AND SINEAD AND TO FIND OUT WHAT THOSE BOTTOM WHIPPING SESSIONS WERE ALL ABOUT...

You went back to the Academy the other night. How was that?
It was weird meeting all of the students who had left. I'd only been away for a couple of days, but it was great to see Ainslie and Sinead.

Did you feel sad seeing them?
In a way. I think I would have preferred seeing them when they got out so I could talk to them properly. I had to follow the rules and couldn't say certain things, so for me it would have been easier if I could speak freely and have a craic. It did make me realise I would love to have still been there, but needless to say I'm not.

How did you feel when you were expelled?
I'd prepared myself for it. I was a bit gutted, but I looked around at Sinead and Ainslie and said "good luck" to them. They were my rock in there, they were my mates. From the very beginning I bonded with both of them, and my relationships with them built and built. Being up against those two was a comfort because I really wanted them to do well. Also, getting voted off meant I didn't have to choose between them on the vote. I wouldn't have been able to do that. I might have put both their names down!

Were you disappointed that David or Lemar didn't vote for you?
I wasn't expecting them to. I was disappointed to a certain extent, but Ainslie and myself are two totally different musical genres and when

you're in that studio and Ainslie is performing, there's nothing like him. I'm more of a balladeer. I sing and let the song do the work. Ainslie is amazing so I can't be disappointed. But it was comforting that there was such a small number of votes between Sinead and me.

Have you been recognised since you've been out?
Yes, people have been asking for autographs and stuff. Obviously I love all the attention! It's so nice that people like me and I've been perceived well. When you're in there it's one of the worries that you have. I wondered what the public thought of me and what the papers had been saying. But I've been really lucky.

How are things between you and Sinead now?
I think the world of her, we got really close. We had a snog and we both thought that was it, but everyone's made a really big deal about it. I didn't treat her differently to anyone else – even Ainslie and I had a hug. But we never kissed!

Do you think you'll get together?
Obviously there is an attraction there. I've been out for a few days and I look back on our time together with such affection. We'll see what happens. We intend to meet up and I know that whatever happens we'll be really good friends.

Did you buy her the ring you gave to her?
No, I bought myself a ring for my pinkie. She liked it so I said she could have it. It was only a pound!

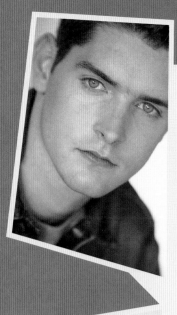

You took your mikes off so you could have a chat the other night, didn't you?

We did. What were they going to do, expel me? I had a few words with her and Ainslie as I knew the two of them had been down in the dumps. I think the pressure on them is major and I'd like to think it's because they're missing me as well! So I wanted to say to stay focused and do their best and not worry about me. I was worried about them. Things were said to Ainslie that night which I wasn't happy about.

Marli and Chris encouraged him to leave, didn't they?

Yes, I was so annoyed at that. Ainslie seems a bit crazy but he's a bit soft as well, he would really worry about something like that. He worries about what people will think of him. For them to say that to him… I was absolutely fuming. He took me outside and we sat on our bench and he told me. I felt like saying to them: "What's that all about?" But I didn't want to make an issue of it.

Why do you think they said it?

I have a notion it's jealousy. Ainslie has such a major chance of winning this competition.

Do you think Ainslie will win?

I want Sinead or Ainslie to win, but I think Sinead or David will win. I think Lemar will be under pressure at this week's Live Showdown. David has had a hard time with coming in late and being on probation and that raises your profile. Sinead is the same; she's been on probation and won public votes and has a big fan base. Lemar has never been on probation, he lost the Radio One vote and he's been a quiet figure. I think because he's so good, people won't vote for him because they'll think everyone else will. I think if Ainslie survives this week, he has a very good chance of going on to

the top deck. I think David and Sinead will have the public votes, then Sinead will go for Ainslie and David will go for Lemar. Then I don't know which way Richard Park will go. He gets the final draw if there's a vote.

Who do you think will go on to be the biggest star despite who wins?

Probably me! Seriously though, I think Lemar will. I think Ainslie will be a close second. But I think everyone who's left will make it because they're brilliant. Just as long as they don't lose themselves. It's very easy to do that because you're getting a lot of attention, but next week there will be another reality TV programme and there will be somebody else to watch. We've got to stay focused and realise that we're not any better now, we've just got a bigger profile. There's a lot of work ahead if we want any success.

Did you fancy any of the other girls in the Academy apart from Sinead?

At the very beginning I quiet fancied Camilla, but that left after a couple of weeks. I think she's a beautiful girl, but features only go so far. Katie is very attractive too and she's very witty.

You hadn't travelled much before Fame Academy. Has the whole being in London and being on TV experience been scary?

It's funny, but I've taken it all in my stride. I lived in Belfast in a house with eight people for half a year, which was good training. The fact that I haven't left home doesn't really matter.

Are you missing Ainslie a lot?

I am. I went to bed last night and the last thing I thought of was Ainslie because I was watching him on TV, sitting on our bench talking to me. We'll always be friends. Once he's out we can build on the friendship that we have.

At what point did you become so close?

We could laugh at each other from the first week and once we got to talk a bit more about friends and family we found that we had a lot in common. By the third week we were inseparable. I know all about his friends and family and he knows all about mine, so we would talk about them as if we knew them.

Do you miss your bench chats?

I do. On Wednesday night he took me out onto the bench and said: "Oh Mali, I never thought we'd be back on this bench." And I said: "I bet you never thought you'd hear this again?" And I lifted up me leg and went "paaaaaarrrrppp"! It was so funny. It was a wee bit emotional, actually.

Are you planning to release any of the songs you wrote together, like 'Bad Bad Butcher'?

The way I see if, if the Cheeky Girls can do well with their song we've got a good chance. I'm going for a Christmas Number One with 'Bad Bad Butcher'. The response we've got from 'Bad Bad Butcher' and 'Fine Waitresses' is amazing. Some of the verses got a bit X-rated, but it would be nice to do something with them.

Is there anything you wish people hadn't seen while you were in Fame Academy?

I wish they hadn't seen my pecker. Or the whipping stuff. But I don't really have any regrets, thank God. I thought people might shout abuse at me about things I'd done, but no-one's said anything.

What was the whipping all about?

The flower stems were really hard so Ainslie decided it would be a good experiment for me to give him a whip. And obviously he had to do it back to me! It was sore, but it was hilarious. I actually drew blood from Ainslie's cheek. He'll have a scar for life. It'll be something for his girlfriend to rub cream into.

Did you mind people seeing you kiss Sinead?

I didn't mind at all. We'd had a few drinks, we snogged, people do it all the time. I was just disappointed it was only 37 seconds, but she's quite a good kisser, actually.

What was your best moment in the Academy?

There are so many. I could list a hundred moments with Ainslie and Sinead. But I would say working with Lionel Ritchie has to be the best. He was very inspirational because he was so willing to share his knowledge and guide us. He's a real gentleman.

Do you think there's real rivalry between Ainslie and David?

It may have been slightly blown out of proportion. I think the fact that David said he wanted to out-perform Ainslie didn't help things. I think that was a mistake.

What are your plans for the future?

We've got the Fame Academy album coming out, of course there's the tour and I'd like a solo career in music. Folk has always been my mainstay and somebody has said I'll be the modern face of folk music. But I don't want to be branded like that. I would like the added bonus of going in a more contemporary direction. I think the Van Morrisons of this world are fantastic; that's what I would like to go into. It's all looking very positive, so we'll see. The most important thing for me right now is to go home and spend some time with my family. And I'm going to look back on some of the footage as well. I haven't seen the whipping yet, so I'm quite looking forward to watching that!

Interview
Richard

WE MET UP WITH RICHARD AT HALF-TERM AND HE HAD A PRETTY GOOD IDEA OF WHO WAS GOING TO WIN THE FAME ACADEMY BATTLE FOR THE BIG PRIZE.

How are you finding Fame Academy?

It's not easy, because every day brings new issues. The students have huge ups and downs depending on whether they think they're in or out of favour. And the teachers are not dissimilar. We all have bad mornings where we have different views about the students and I think it's going to get even more difficult the less students we have. There will be a real levelling out in the perceived standard by the public. Some people here can write, sing and dance so because of what Fame Academy stands for they should be the favourites to win. But it doesn't always work out like that because it's not down to the week's work in the Academy, it's down to the Friday night performance. We are going to have to be so precise in our assessments all the time. The wrong choice will change everything.

Do you find it hard picking the students' performances apart?

It's very tough and we will never satisfy everybody. Teachers take baggage with them, so you will always remember students being late or being rude and you bring that to the grading table.

Who is your favourite to win?

It's looking to me like David or Sinead. Sinead is really tenacious and has good songs and sings them extremely well. David is a charmer with songwriting ability and a very good voice. I think they may well make the final with any other person from the group. Ainslie is the most individual because he's the most rocker-ish, but he might not be the best person to win a competition. Lemar is very much on top of one field of music, but charismatically he's coming up a bit short at the moment, which may affect him. Nigel wouldn't be a popular choice in the teaching room, but I don't discount him and exactly the same can be said of Katie. This whole programme will be worth watching just to see Katie go from nothing to something. Unfortunately I think it is beyond Malachi to win, but I think he's a great guy.

Which of the students do you think will be the biggest star?

History relates that in these talent shows a couple of people come out and make it, but it's not always the winner. Will Young has gone up and down a bit versus Gareth and they seem to have decided to go about together. If David was the winner and Ainslie was second, I couldn't see them doing that. Both of those have star quality, Nigel has star quality in clubland and Katie has star quality in a pop star way. Sinead is short of star quality, but then so in a sense are people like Alanis Morrisette. Week by week people will be exposed as not being right. I think we've got to wait and see.

Who do you think would be most suited to the pop star lifestyle?

Ainslie. He'll be there drinking the beer and doing the lot. He'll be out there with the babes in the back of the limo, staggering into his flat with his agent reminding him that he's got to fly to New York in the morning. I think he certainly thinks he'd be very suited to it, but we've still got to find out if he has the talent for it.

Do you ever feel guilty about how hard you work the students?

Never, because when you are out on the road as a pop star, you work so hard. Take Atomic Kitten or Blue; these people are working 18-20 hours a day because they want to maximise their opportunities over what history tells us is a relatively brief period of time. It is in everyone's interests to work hard. They can sleep later. We are trying to encourage eight hours sleep a night, but I don't think we're getting it because there's a lot of horseplay at night. Sadly there's no rule about whipping each others' bottoms.

Who's been the biggest rule breaker?

Ainslie is ahead in breaking the rules, but overall there haven't been that many rules broken. We never said we weren't going to drink; we're adults. We also never said people couldn't smoke, although they do have to smoke outside, but I think Ainslie has been encouraging other people to smoke, which isn't great. Malachi has pushed the boundaries a bit and everybody else has had their moments with food fights and stuff, which I wasn't happy about. I've had to draw a line between what is blatant rule breaking and letting off steam in this environment. It's like boarding school in a way; you have to do that.

Some people have got off quite lightly with punishments, though...

If I get too hung up on the rules I will curtail creativity, which I don't want to do. I think the way we've done it is about right.

Are you pleased with your team of teachers?

Absolutely. Kevin is a very nice man and a bit of a tough guy. Carrie Grant is a supreme professional, bordering on perfectionist. And Jo is a top class arranger and all round lovely person. Pam Sheyne has written a number one hit and her credentials are there on paper. She's bringing out the best in people who couldn't, until now, write great songs. Jeremy is also a lovely man and very popular with the students.

Let's go through all the students and you can let us know what you think the future holds for them...

Ainslie – I think Ainslie wants to put a rock band together and be the frontman and leading songwriter. I think what he's doing in here is proving a love of music and showing that he writes very good songs. I'm expecting him to have a song that he's written in the charts next year.

Malachi – Malachi has a beautiful - if typical - Irish folksy voice and is better suited to soft ballads. He isn't as good on the powerful songs. He's become a better stage performer but is not likely to be the winner. His career will depend on how much he realises his strengths and weaknesses and how plausible he thinks he'll be as a pop star. Through Kevin's training he's developing as a good-looking bloke and some modelling agents are interested in him. So he – and other students – might end up in a situation they never dreamt of.

Pippa – Pippa is a very nice person and sings well at times, but not always. She's not really a songwriter, but I think she's found a look that suits her in the Academy – short tops and tight jeans. She might be very suited to a dance record, if not the kind of song Mariah Carey would sing. But there is something there.

Marli – Marli came in here as a highly talented individual. Age wise, she's a little older than people who are trying to break into the business and get a record released tend to be these days. She's a good songwriter but probably not yet a brilliant one. She is looking great but time is not on her side, so it needs to happen for her quite quickly. She is a lovely, caring person and it's a shame her record deals haven't come off for her in the past.

Katie – Katie has come from being the back marker on the day the students arrived on the Academy. But the way she carries herself on and off of stage and the way she sings songs has changed immensely. She's even showing that songwriting is not completely beyond her. There are many young pop stars in the world who aren't more talented than Katie, so it's all going to depend on how far she stretches herself. I can't predict how far that will be.

Nigel – There is an album there if the record company involved in the project want to go along with it. I think he could do ten very strong covers, a couple of songs that have been written for him and a couple that he's written himself.

David – He is certainly looking like a potential winner as he sings brilliantly and he writes original songs cleverly. He's an all round good guy whom I've no doubt has a few moods, but hasn't really shown them yet. He looks the part and it's hard to find any flaws with him except he's almost too good to be true. He's a little bit "Disney", but he's certainly in the winners enclosure.

Lemar – Lemar's strengths are a very nice style and a good voice and he's proved himself good at singing covers. He's also a good student and is a very nice chap. But the downside is that he can be un-charismatic, too breathy and occasionally he has problems with tone and plods a bit. But he could do well with the right song. His destiny is in his own hands.

Naomi – I think we never really found out what Naomi had to offer. It looked to me like she was an extremely good singer and like a female Malachi. Whether she had the depth to drive herself up to the winning post? I doubt it.

Chris – He was a lot of people's favourite before the show but I thought he was a bit of a lightweight. He was perfectly cast as a Butlin's redcoat. He's nice, bright and cheery and doesn't let anything get to him, but I never saw him as the winner.

Sinead – I'm a big fan; she's absolutely unfazed by anything. There's a recording studio waiting for her and I think she'll be huge in Ireland. With her attitude, I don't think she can fail. She is exceptional in everything she does and she has never let herself down.

Ashley – If I were him I wouldn't have entered this competition because I don't think he's right for it. I think giving up his job in order to search out the stardom he craves was extremely brave of him, but I don't think he ever looked like he was going to be the winner in either singing or songwriting.

Camilla – Camilla is extremely talented in my view, but she's not suited to the lifestyle of the Academy. I think she could do stage shows, I'm very confident that's where she should head. She has a shot at stardom in some shape or form. If she wants to be in showbiz, it beckons.

Week Nine

Saturday

The students are to be teamed up with top songwriters this afternoon. "We're aiming to write songs that can be performed in the final Live Showdown and released as singles" advises Pam. Ainslie is delighted when he discovers that he will be working with his musical heroes, Mark and Saul from James. Sinead will be working with duo Pete Glenister and Deni Lew, who helped launch Darius's career, David will team up with John McLaughlin and Steve Duberry, who have worked with Liberty X, Five and Billie, while Lemar will be working with the Academy's super-writer Pam and Geoffrey Williams, who has written for Michael Jackson and 90s boy group Color Me Badd. David gets back after his appearance on 'The Saturday Show' and excitedly tells the other students about his star-studded morning, during which he met Ms Dynamite and Westlife (who recognised him!). The students and teachers gather to watch footage of last night's Live Showdown. Lemar tells The Head he is unhappy about the comments he made about his performance. "The comment you made on the night was it was "uninspiring." I thought that was really rubbish, I genuinely did. It was a throwaway comment". After much discussion, they agree to disagree, but when Richard leaves, Lemar tells Ainslie that he's glad he had his say.

That evening, the students, teachers and songwriters regroup for an acoustic session and showcase the tracks they've been working on. Ainslie sings 'Take My Time', Sinead presents 'I Can't Break Down', Lemar follows with 'Make Tonight Beautiful' and finally David sings 'Don't Walk Away'.

Jeremy announces they will be having a grand "Sumo" competition and the winner will go to the pub. After much pushing, shoving and grunting, Ainslie is named the surprise winner and disappears to the pub with Sinead. They return from the pub quite tipsy and Ainslie's drunken singing wakes Lemar, who pipes up with a helium-fuelled version 'Pigeon Boy'.

Sunday

Lemar and a cold-ridden Sinead read through the copy of OK! Magazine which the students are starring in, when the songwriters arrive for another session. Lemar chats to his co-writers about how weird he's finding being a celebrity. Geoffrey gives him some sound advice, saying: "People look at you the way they choose to look at you. The only thing you can control is how you're being. That's all you can do."

After the songwriters leave, David discusses his performance on last Friday's Live Showdown with Carrie. "There's a lot of room for improvement. If I were you, I wouldn't be happy with that performance," she tells the shocked Scot. "At the end of the day. I've only got two weeks left –
if that – how much can I do?" he asks. "You can do loads if you're willing," says Carrie firmly.

Sinead has a vocal session with Carrie, who thinks her song for this Friday's Live Showdown is sounding fantastic. Sinead admits she's really missing Malachi but although she does like him, she wants to keep him on his toes!

Lemar, David and Sinead chat about the show's prize. David says if his music career falters he'll go back to University. Sinead confides to David that she'll be going to visit Malachi at Christmas. Ainslie is literally climbing the walls with boredom and attempts to scale a wall in the living room. After falling down he tries to lift a glass cabinet which is covering a saxophone, but is spotted by the Academy cameras and a warning "Don't even think about it" comes over the tannoy.

Kevin chases Ainslie around the Academy begging him to stop smoking. Ainslie laughs and goes for a cigarette anyway. The students spend the evening painting each other's faces whilst singing comedy Christmas songs. As you do.

Monday

Carrie chats to the students in the lounge and tells an unhappy David that he can change his song for the Live Showdown if he doesn't like it.

SINEAD

ON PROBATION

Kevin kicks off the dance class with a one-minute silence for the much missed Malachi. On Friday night, the students will be singing duets: David and Lemar will cover Stevie Wonder's 'As' and Sinead and Ainslie will perform The Rolling Stones' 'Satisfaction'. Ainslie borrows a pair of Sinead's pants as he's run out of clean ones. After parading around in the tight black numbers whilst talking to himself, he announces: "I think I'll wear these buggers. I've run out of my own pants!"

The students visit the Royal Free Hospital. Autographs are signed, photos are taken, questions are asked and smiles are huge. David switches on the Fame Academy Christmas lights and the group sing 'Silent Night' before relaxing with a beer. Jeremy tells the students that following their success at raising money for Children In Need they will be doing a whistlestop tour of Glasgow, Belfast and London to try to raise more cash after Friday's show. Ainslie is excited, but worried that he might not still be around and he's also concerned that his hometown is the only one they're not planning to visit! Sinead reveals to Kevin that Malachi whispered something in her ear before he left the stage last Friday. Kevin smiles and says: "Even at that moment when his dreams are over, he's still got a couple of words for the mighty Quinn." Tucked up in bed, the students discuss what they'll do if their musical careers go belly up. Ainslie plans to become an actor, Sinead would be like to be a street juggler, while David likes the idea of becoming a vet.

Tuesday

The students seem a bit down, so Kevin plays Agony Aunt at the beginning of the dance class. It turns out Ainslie has a problem with his eye, Lemar's hip is playing up, Sinead's feeling podgy, but David is A-OK!

There will also be another BBC Choice sing-off this week. The students will perform their allotted duets, and the winners will get VIP tickets to see The Doves at Brixton Academy tonight. Both Ainslie and David are desperate to win, but who will be the victor? David and Lemar rehearse their duet with Jo. They are determined to win the coveted gig prize, as are Ainslie and Sinead who practice with Jo straight afterwards. The duo are having problems deciding what to sing and consider 10CC's 'I'm Not In Love' and James's 'Sit Down' before deciding on Oasis's 'Don't Look Back In Anger'. But will they stick to their choice?

It's time for the BBC Choice show and David and Lemar are up first, followed by Sinead and Ainslie who decide to stick to the script and sing 'Satisfaction'. When Vanessa announces that Ainslie and Sinead have won, they hop in a limo and make their way to the gig while David falls to the floor shouting: "Damn it! Damn it!" David tells Jo he doesn't care about the vote as long as he's not expelled on Friday. Sinead goes straight to bed when she gets home from the concert, but an inebriated Ainslie attacks the Christmas tree before starting a huge food fight with Kevin. Who's going to clean that up in the morning?!

Wednesday

Sinead is hungover, but all Ainslie is worried about is the mess he made in the lounge and dining room last night. He starts to clear up and Kevin and a fragile Sinead assist. Richard summons a worried Ainslie to his office and stresses how disappointed he is: "You know those fine, fine waitresses? You made those people cry", he tells him. Ainslie is appalled by his behaviour and says: "I took it far too far last night, and I won't take it anywhere near that again."

Sinead chats to Jeremy and gives Malachi a message via a camera, saying: "Hi, Lady Muck here, miss you so much!" In Hampstead, a crowd have gathered to see the students switch on Christmas lights and sing. Back at the Academy they discover all the expelled students have returned to celebrate the launch of the Fame Academy album. There is much kissing and hugging when the current pupils discover their old friends. The students are even more excited when Richard announces a three venue stadium tour for next year with further dates to be

confirmed.

Marli and Chris encourage a confused looking Ainslie to leave the Academy, telling him he doesn't need it to survive in the music business. Lemar drunkenly gatecrashes Malachi's rendition of 'Vincent' on a BBC Choice show and Jo makes him a coffee to help him sober up. "Why do they give me drink? It's so stupid!" Lemar wails to the music pro.

Malachi and Sinead talk about having babies when they leave the Academy and desperately search for somewhere to be on their own. They settle on a sofa in the corridor and take off their mikes so they can whisper privately, then hide under Sinead's hat for a sneaky kiss. Malachi gives Sinead a ring he's wearing and she claims it is "pure gorgeous", but a spoilsport message comes over the tannoy telling the naughty lovebirds to put their microphones back on.

Malachi and Ainslie sit on their favourite bench and admit they've missed each other. Ainslie washes up after dinner as punishment for his behaviour last night. He apologises profusely to the waitresses and tells the chef: "It's an absolute pleasure to meet you. Your meals have been absolutely gorgeous!" Marli tells David she wants him to win Fame Academy so they can have a huge party and also invites herself to his home for New Year. After flirting all night, Lemar and Camilla sneak off to the downstairs toilet for what they think is a secret snog, but the kissing noises are caught on tape and Ainslie later tells Lemar off for being so indiscreet. The students groove to the Fame Academy album in the dance studio, where Katie tells Lemar she has met his girlfriend and thinks she's lovely, but Camilla interrupts the conversation. A touch of jealousy, perchance? The students eventually go to bed, with the expelled students bedding down in sleeping bags on the studio floor.

Thursday

Richard, Carrie and Kevin have a chat about the four remaining students. They all agree that Sinead is having a great week and that Ainslie and David have been very competitive lately, but Kevin feels that David is back to being himself again. They also feel that Lemar has finally found his true self and are happy that Ainslie has coped well without his pal Malachi.

The students rehearse for the Live Showdown and Carrie gets, like, 'deep' when David sings George Michael's 'Freedom'. "People finally understand who you are David, and to you that's freedom," she says.

Ronan Keating arrives at the Academy for the latest Masterclass. Carrie leads him to the practice room where the students perform 'Lullaby'. "Fantastic!" Ronan smiles when it's over. "Brilliant. There's a band right there in front of you. Leave it at that!" Ronan offers some advice about press attention: "Dealing with the media is hard, but you have to laugh it off. Take any of it on board and it will affect you." When the Masterclass is over, Carrie slips away to a secret cupboard and gives Ronan a rocking horse and other gifts for his children. "Way hey. Daddy's coming home with presents tonight!" he grins.

Sinead and Ronan rehearse their duet and the Irish superstar is very pleased: "That was fantastic, well done," Ronan tells Sinead when they finish. The students pack a small bag for the Local Heroes tour, as they won't return to the Academy until late Saturday night. The students give their probation speeches. Ainslie goes first, stating: "I've got the feeling that tomorrow will be my last night. I'm not usually that good at getting to know people, and you've been good people to practice that with. Thanks." David is feeling upbeat. "I'm not going to miss any of you – 'cos I'm going to see you all next week! We're all mates – that's the way it's going to stay." Lemar says: "This has been the best week for me, to share this time with you guys. I've made five, six, seven or eight extremely close friends."

A reluctant Sinead is last, and keeps her speech short and sweet. "I'd like to stay in for the last week 'cos I'd like to do an original song. That would be my dream."

For one student, this is their last night in the Academy. But who's it going to be?

DAVID
HAS PROBABLY MADE THE MOST PROGRESS OF ANYONE IN THE ACADEMY
CARRIE

LEMAR HE'S FUNNY AND HE'S HAVING A GOOD TIME WHILE WORKING HARD
KEVIN

ON PROBATION

Sing for Survival

IT'S THE PENULTIMATE LIVE SHOWDOWN AND THERE'S A CHRISTMASSY VIBE IN THE STUDIO, WITH TINSEL EDGED BANNERS BEING WAVED AROUND FURIOUSLY. THERE ARE ONLY FOUR STUDENTS LEFT AND TENSIONS ARE RUNNING HIGH. THE FRIENDS AND FAMILY AREA IS THE SMALLEST IT'S EVER BEEN, BUT HAVING NOW SPENT THE PAST NINE WEEKS TOGETHER, THE GROUP ARE SUPPORTIVE TO THE END AND THE RELATIVES HUG EACH OTHER LIKE THEY ARE ONE EXTENDED FAMILY.

The students and teachers arrive and all of the students go directly to the middle of the stage rather than taking their seats at the side. Sinead waves and smiles to her friends and family before playing them a bit of air guitar. David and Lemar stay still, while Ainslie stomps around the stage. He claps his hands and shouts "Come on!" It seems he's keen to get the stressful Showdown over with. Cat and Pat come up the runway and the show starts, with Ronan Keating being introduced to huge cheers. It's time for the four probationers to show what they are capable of and Sinead is up first. After telling Cat: "I never thought I'd get this far," she strides down the stage with her guitar and breaks into Blondie's 'One Way Or Another' in full rock chick mode. Disaster strikes when her guitar strap breaks, but like a true professional she carries on regardless. Carrie is full of praise. "It was absolutely brilliant!" she grins.

Lemar is next and dedicates his Survival Song, Prince's 'Nothing Compares 2 U', to "my girl Charmaine." Cat makes a comment about the "Romance in the Academy" during the week, referring to his and Camilla's snog, but Lemar decides to let his song do the talking. Richard is clearly impressed. "He sang better than he's ever sung before," he says. Cat questions Lemar about his and Richard's cross words after last weeks' Showdown, but Lemar says simply: "There's love there, man. It's all good."

Back on stage Ainslie waits to perform his Survival Song, U2's 'With Or Without You'. He strolls up the stage with his guitar and soon has everyone singing along, apart from his brother who is standing very still with his hand on his chest looking proud. The Head declares: "Ainslie's really engaging. I think he will make it into that recording studio."

The final probationer to perform is David and Cat asks him if he's feeling pressured. "I don't feel any pressure. I'm here by default. The fact I'm here is mind-blowing for me," is his honest answer. He coolly strolls down the

runway with his hands in his pockets and launches into George Michael's 'Freedom'. All the teachers smile when he starts working the audience: "I'm really proud of him tonight," says Carrie when he's finished. Patrick asks Jeremy about the Ainslie/David rivalry and Jeremy admits he doesn't think they always get on brilliantly. Ainslie and David both look confused, then furious. "Is he talking about us? Shut up!" Ainslie shouts from the stage, while David responds testily: "I'm fed up with all this rubbish about Ainslie. Me and Ainslie are mates, that's all there is."

The audience vote results are in and with 33% Lemar is the clear winner. Ainslie is next with 26%, followed by Sinead with 22% and finally David with 19%. David looks disappointed and hangs his head. It's time for the duets and Sinead and Ainslie are up first with The Rolling Stones' 'Satisfaction'. Carrie admits she's never seen Sinead as confident as she is tonight. David and Lemar perform their rendition of Stevie Wonder's 'As', and round the song off with a hug. Carrie thinks working with Lemar has helped David find a new side to his voice. "I think working with Lemar has turned him into a little soul brother. That was fantastic!" she gushes. With all the students gathered back on the stage, Cat announces that the Fame Academy album already has pre-sales of 250,000, meaning it's achieved Gold status before it's even been released. Ronan comes on and presents a Gold Disk to the students and jokes: "I hope they're being paid for it!" Ronan stays on stage while a band assembles behind him because it's time for his and Sinead's duet of his Number One hit, 'If Tomorrow Never Comes'. He smiles when Sinead starts singing, obviously blown away by her crystal clear voice. Afterwards Sinead is overjoyed, especially when Ronan hugs and thanks her.

It's that tough time of the show when the teachers have to name who they think has performed best. Pam and Carrie choose Sinead, Richard goes for Ainslie, while Kevin picks David. Then it's time for the students to hear their fate as they discover who has been saved in the public vote. Over 2.2 million votes have been cast, but who are the two favourites? "Saved by the public and going into the Fame Academy final is... " Cat begins as silence descends upon the studio, "Sinead!" Sinead looks absolutely amazed, but not as stunned as David who is open mouthed and wide eyed when Cat tells him that he's also in the final. His mum thrusts her fists into the air, and David shouts: "I'm in the final!" Sinead and David take their places to vote for the student they want to stay. The atmosphere is strained, and Ainslie and Lemar joke around on stage to lighten the mood. Both Sinead and David admit they've voted on tonight's performance, and both vote for Lemar, meaning that showman, rebel, and all round rock'n'roll star Ainslie is going home. When it's announced that he's been expelled, his mum and brother rush towards the stage to see him, but Pat stops them getting on stage just in time. "My head's going 'aaargggghhhhhh!'" Ainslie admits,"It's a strange feeling. I expected this all day, but it still hits you right in the balls when it comes!" He looks absolutely gutted and hugs Patrick. "There's the Princess!" the presenter exclaims, pointing to Bernadette who is waiting at the other end of the stage runway. Ainslie covers his face as he walks quickly towards his girlfriend and gives her a huge hug. The teachers swiftly get up and leave the studio, obviously keen to have a few words with Ainslie themselves.

When the show is finished, the Fame Academy tour bus awaits to take the students on their whistlestop tour. Upstairs in the BBC Choice studio Ainslie is being interviewed by Vanessa and Danaan and gives one last performance of 'With Or Without You'. When the show is over he hugs Bernadette, cheers and shouts: "The cameras are off!"

He may be pleased to have his privacy back now, but we don't reckon it will be long before Ainslie is up and rocking in front of the cameras once again!

Interview
Ainslie

AINSLIE MAY HAVE BEEN THE ACADEMY REBEL, BUT HE ADMITS
HE CRIED LIKE A BABY WHEN HE WAS EXPELLED. STILL,
HIS RECENT GOOD NEWS HAS CERTAINLY CHEERED HIM UP.

How have things been since you got expelled?
My feet haven't touched the ground. I thought the Academy was hard going, but it was a holiday camp in there compared to this. It's insane!

Have you been recognised a lot?
Quite a lot. It's great because it's the eccentric, interesting people who have approached me. They're my favourite kind of people – the weird and strange ones – so I'm really pleased they've become my fans.

How did you feel when you were expelled?
I kind of expected it, but when it came it was an overwhelming mix of emotions. It was excitement at getting out, but a real sadness that the whole experience was over. I was scared about what it would be like coming back into the world.

How was it getting to see your family and your girlfriend The Princess, aka Bernadette?
It was so lovely. I missed a lot of people, so although initially I was gutted at being expelled, as soon as I got to the end of the stage, I was fine.

You covered your face when you walked down. Were you crying or just in shock?
I was crying like a baby and I just didn't want people to see any more tears. They'd seen quite enough already.

You seemed to hate the voting process more than anyone...
I hated it so much. They were people I was bonding with and becoming friends with. I think that's one of the great things about Fame Academy; instead of trying to belittle each other and make ourselves great, we really encouraged each other and tried to make us all brilliant. So to have to go out on Friday night and vote somebody off was really, really hard.

Do you regret any of your voting decisions?
No. I was always forthright in how I felt and I always voted for the person I thought was best.

What's the truth about your and David's rivalry?
Everyone was obsessed with it apart from me and David, who forgot about it after the first fortnight. It was nothing.

Who do you think is going to win Fame Academy?
It's so close. I don't think it will be Lemar, although I would like him to. Some of the songs he's written are so innovative and original; he has a voice like honey in sunshine. His charisma on stage blows me away. But all three of them are brilliant and whoever wins deserves it.

Why did you talk to yourself in the Academy?
I've always done it, it's a way of centering myself, escaping from everybody else, and getting my mind clear. I did it all the time at first and everybody ignored it, but then I realised that everybody was watching, so I toned it down. Sometimes I would be rabbiting on and then realise that the whole nation was watching me.

Is there anything you wish people hadn't seen?
I kinda regret prancing around in girls' pants. Sinead's knickers were alright, but when I got

back from The Doves and I was drunk, I put on these white ones that this girl sent me and I was dancing around the bedroom wearing them and a pink hat. I'm not looking forward to seeing that.

Which performance were you most pleased with?
When I sang 'You Really Got Me' by The Kinks.

Ah yes, when you leapt into the crowd...
Yes. By the time I'd thought about it properly I was lying on the floor. The audience didn't catch me either; they just kind of broke my fall.

Have you seen Malachi since you've been out?
No. I've spoken to him a few times on the phone and we're meeting up tomorrow night and going out on the town. He is the nicest guy, he's probably the funniest person I've ever met.

Did you miss him during your last week?
Desperately. He just had such warmth about him. I'm not a very funny person but I love to laugh, so I tend to hang around with funny people. He really brought out my sense of humour and helped me through the experience a lot. It would have been much harder had he not been there.

Who else were you close to?
Lemar. He's a really genuine guy and we really bonded. I struggle to make close friendships and I've always been a bit of an outsider, so I did really well to have made two new close friends.

Have you thought about buying your and Malachi's bench?
It would be nice. I wonder what will come of it? I might look into it and see if I can buy it.

What did you think when Marli and Chris said you should leave the Academy?
I can kind of see their reasoning. I think they thought it would somehow give me loads of

credibility to walk out. But if being in Fame Academy had ruined my credibility, walking out wasn't going to save it. It made me think: "If you think it ruins your credibility being here, why did you come back for a sleepover?" They didn't make me think about leaving at all. I always knew I would stay there as long as possible.

The Head gave you a few tellings off, but he still seemed to really like you...
Richard was brilliant. He is a very entertaining, charming, pain in the a**e of a man! Although he told me off, I have a lot of respect for him. He knows what he's talking about.

How did you get on with the rest of the teachers?
I couldn't have asked for a better group of tutors. Kevin Adams was such a top guy and his classes were amazing. Everyone moaned about Kevin's classes. I moaned about everything else, but that's the one thing I loved. He's so motivating. Carrie was lovely, Pam was brilliant and Jo Noel is an absolute musical genius. She really took care of me in there, she was really tender and caring. She's incredible.

How did it feel when the teachers said what a good showman you were?
That was great. I thought I would get shot down because I'm not the most technically pitch perfect singer. I think it said something great about Fame Academy that I could be the kind of performer I am

and still be encouraged and valued. Especially by Carrie Grant. She's a vocal coach and should be all about technical accuracy, but she really understood me.

Let's talk through the Academy snogs. Firstly, what did you make of Sinead and Malachi's?

That was great. After it happened Malachi came downstairs and said: "I've just snogged Sinead!" I couldn't believe it, I was really surprised. He'd been trying to snog her the whole time he was in there and I thought there was no way he would do it. I even told him to give up, but his persistence obviously paid off.

Do you think anything more will happen between them?

No, I think they were just having a bit of fun.

What about Marli and Jeremy?

It was a bit mad. It was totally unexpected and I was amazed it happened. They're both free and are consenting adults, so they can do what they want, but I definitely don't think anything else will happen.

Finally, what do you reckon to Camilla and Lemar?

Nothing will happen there. Lemar will feel terrible and Camilla will feel stupid. It was very much a drunken thing. When you've been in the Academy for nine weeks your head doesn't work how it's supposed to. You lose sight of the world and really strange things happen. I know Lemar really regrets it, as it's the last thing he would normally do.

Did the Academy bring out your rebellious side, or are you like that anyway?

The Academy brought it out in me. I'm usually a lot more easy going. I think it was because I was forced back into being a school kid again and I didn't want to do things. I had a lot more attitude in there than I would usually have. Once I'd made a rebellious name for myself, a subconscious part of me wanted to keep it going.

Did you play up to the cameras?

I did a bit. I had lots of fun and I knew people were watching. I'm an exhibitionist and if the cameras hadn't been there I would probably have been an exhibitionist for the sake of the people in the Academy.

Tell us about your good news?

I've been signed by Mercury Records. It's an album deal – my single will come out in February and the album should be out next summer. It's amazing. It's exactly how I would have wanted things to happen. I didn't go into Fame Academy thinking I was going to win it. I wanted to go in there, get a showcase, then come out and get a record deal; and that's happened. I couldn't be happier.

What's the single going to be like?

I'm releasing 'Keep Me a Secret'. I think Lemar is going to take 'Lullaby' – I think that's going to be his single – and I'm really proud to have been a part of both of those songs. I'm going to get to write most of the new album as well.

You were in a band before that didn't make it. Did you ever feel like giving up on music?

No. I've tried doing other things, and it turns out I'm awful at everything else. Whatever happens, I'll always be doing music.

So what happens now?

I'm going into the studio, getting my album recorded and making sure it's the best I can possibly make it. I'm so excited!

Yearbook

JUDGING BY THE YEARBOOK ENTRIES THEY DID DURING THEIR FIRST WEEK IN THE ACADEMY, IF THE STUDENTS' MUSICAL CAREERS GO BELLY UP THEY CAN ALWAYS DON HEADSCARVES AND BECOME FORTUNE TELLERS ON BRIGHTON PIER. THEN AGAIN, THEY DID GET A FEW THINGS WRONG.

The predictions

So right!

Marli will snog Ainslie/Jeremy
Katie's best friend will be Marli
Sinead is most likely to remain mysterious
Sinead will snog Malachi and he'll be her best friend
Camilla will snog Lemar
Ainslie is most likely to break the rules
Chris is most likely to look in the mirror
Malachi is most likely to make everyone laugh and snog
Sinead/anyone
Nigel will cry when he sees his wife and kids
David is most likely to smile and his best friend will be Nigel

So wrong!

Katie will snog Kevin
Pippa will snog Lemar
Ainslie will snog Naomi/Marli/anyone
Chris will snog the blonde camerawoman
Chris will cry when he wins
Nigel will snog Katie
David will snog Katie/Nigel

Regrets, they've had a few...

Here's what the students predicted each other would regret most about their time in the Academy

Marli ▸ Not performing her own songs
Naomi ▸ Stressing about her voice
Katie ▸ Mentioning her daily poo
Sinead ▸ Not telling Malachi how she felt
Pippa ▸ Her lack of confidence
Camilla ▸ Using the free lip gloss
Ainslie ▸ Will regret nothing
Chris ▸ Not letting himself go
Malachi ▸ Not being able to dance
Nigel ▸ Stressing out
Lemar ▸ Will regret nothing
Ashley ▸ Not having confidence in himself
David ▸ Cleaning his backside on Malachi's pillow(!)

DAVID

HE COULD BE
A BILLY JOEL
OF TODAY
PAM

HIS
TRANSFORMATION
HAS BEEN
INCREDIBLE...
A BEAUTIFUL,
SOULFUL VOICE
CARRIE

COULD WIN IF HE
GIVES A MASTERFUL
PERFORMANCE
KEVIN

SINGING TO WIN

Saturday

Straight after the Showdown, David, Sinead and Lemar jump on to the bright purple Fame Academy tour bus for the Local Heroes tour and start the 420 mile overnight journey to Glasgow. They grab a few hours kip in bunks, but all too soon Jeremy is waking them and they have to get made up and into costume for their first gig of the day. As it's David's hometown he comes out last to perform 'Living a Lie' to a huge crowd of screaming fans who have surfaced at 8.30am to see their local hero. It's over to Belfast by plane next, for Sinead to wow her legions of fans. There are lots of posters being waved for the Irish lass and an enormous amount of people cram into the city centre at 1.30pm to welcome Sinead plus special guest, Malachi! Finally, a private jet whisks the team to Lakeside Shopping Centre for a 7.30pm kick-off in London, where Jeremy introduces Lemar to his public and the noise levels reach an eardrum shattering volume. It's a short trip home to the Academy and for the exhausted group, the realisation of being the three surviving students hits home when they see the rest of the beds have been taken away, leaving just their own in the large dormitory.

No superstar perks are laid on for the group, as they have to lug their own cases up the stairs and everyone has an early night. Sinead is too exhausted to take her make-up off and Lemar manages to quickly update his web diary before they turn the lights out at 11.30pm. All things considered, it's been a hectic 24 hours for this tired, but satisfied bunch.

Sunday

Carrie wakes the students at 8.30am and is met by a chorus of grunts, yawns and moans. She encourages them out of bed by reminding them that they are now experiencing the reality of a popstar lifestyle: they may get just one day off after six months of the sort of timetable they had yesterday. The Showdown post-mortem is too much for Lemar, who can hardly keep his eyes open, but he's awake enough to be pleased with both his performances and Richard concedes it was "much better than last week". Carrie describes Sinead's version of 'One Way or Another' as her "best performance, totally gutsy", but Richard takes his life in his hands by saying he thought it was "vocally, a bit flat". Sinead is just happy to have kept it all under control after her guitar strap broke. David gets some of his best reviews yet and describes how he got really lost in the moment when he sang 'Freedom'. "Two great performances (from David) on Friday...could this be enough for people to think 'he could be on the George Michael plane'?" muses Richard. So, it's good news all around, but the Head is quick to remind them "Next week you'll be singing to win."

David and Sinead are taken to Abbey Road Studios to record videos for their single releases should they win. As Lemar is temporarily at a loose end, Jeremy presents him with a video camera to record a tour of the Academy: "It's something you'll be able to show your grandchildren" Jeremy enthuses, to a somewhat bewildered looking Lemar. He whizzes through the Academy, giving a commentary on each room, camera and statue, reminiscing on events that took place in every location. Carrie promises to let the students in on some of the background gossip once the show is over: "One day I'll tell you all the stories from behind the scenes" she teases. Later that evening, David gets a surprise phone call of support from ex-student Nigel. "You've got to win it – pull out all the stops. The kids think you're great, they can't wait to meet their Uncle David!" After that, David just can't stop smiling!

Monday

Kevin takes the three remaining students out to Ainslie's favourite bench to offer up a minute's silence for their old pal. "Last week we suffered a great loss. Brother Ainslie, rebel of the

Academy will be sorely missed" intones Kevin. It's Carrie's turn to gee up some competitive spirit in the ranks, by encouraging the students to think of this week as a political campaign. "The voting is incredibly close. You have to motivate your people to pick up the phone" she tells them decisively. The group of friends are unwilling to get too competitive however, so it looks like it's up to their supporters to fight it out for them.

Local school children excitedly descend on the Academy that afternoon to win the chance of a tour inside and to meet the students. The five lucky winners get shown around, have a boogie in the dance studio and listen to a special performance of 'Lullaby'. There's a massive autograph signing stint as well as lots of general fan/student adoration and it's hard to know who enjoys themselves more; the delighted fans or the finalists. "That was great!" shouts Lemar afterwards.

Cabin fever strikes again that evening and David and Lemar storm the BBC Choice studio to support Ainslie as he performs 'Keep Me a Secret' live. Ainslie is delighted to see them and grins as he sings, probably chuffed that they are following his example and breaking some rules! There's a flurry of phone calls to break the monotony, but boredom soon reigns again and it's back to favourite japes such as sliding down the bannisters, faking an escape and breaking into Jeremy's office to make prank phone calls. It's all fun and games now, but they're going to be tired again in the morning...

Tuesday

Kevin is jack-of-all-trades today, as he not only does the morning workout, but takes Carrie's vocal warm-up and runs through the individual performances for Friday night. Both he and David remind Lemar to keep his eyes open while he's singing and to smile more so that the audience can really connect with him. "I was smiling" pleads a very tired looking Lemar.

Four more BBC Choice competition winners come to the Academy for a tour and get a personal rendition of 'Lean On Me'. They also get to have a Q&A with the three students and a photo session in the lounge. Each of the students then has an interview with Radio 1, giving them an opportunity to persuade the public to vote for them in best party political broadcast style.

Sinead is thrilled to get a call from Malachi and happily bounces around the dining room saying "my heart's pounding!". More excitement ensues when Carrie announces that 'The Sun' newspaper want to do a photoshoot with all the students dressed up as their favourite pop idols. David decides to be John Lennon, Sinead will become Madonna and Lemar wants to be Stevie Wonder, but is being heavily persuaded to do a Lenny Kravitz instead!

That evening all three watch their original audition tapes and Sinead cringes at her bum notes in 'Back for Good'; a song she learnt on the drive from Irvinestown to Belfast. David laughs at his famous facial contortions, shrieking "Look at mah eyebrows!" and Lemar is pretty happy about his singing, if not his small talk with the interviewers. Carrie is obviously pleased with her little posse's progress, however, stating: "I'm really proud of you because I can see how hard you've all worked."

Superstar R'n'B soul singer Beverley Knight has made a special request to have a guest artist on her tour this Monday. Our boy Lemar is going to be onstage at the Hammersmith Apollo with the lady herself and he is quite happy about it: "You're taking the mick! Aaaaaahhhhh!!!" he yells. Following all the excitement, Jeremy tries to calm the group down with a selection of recent press cuttings for them to peruse. The gang enjoy reading how Lemar's local newspaper are running a 'Make Lemar a Star' campaign, that David has almost daily news articles in his town's paper and that there is Sinead merchandise including t-shirts being made to drum up support for her in Ireland.

LEMAR

I LOVE HIM TO BITS. HE'S INCREDIBLY TALENTED AND HE'LL GO FAR
PAM

HIS VOICE IS HIS BEST INSTRUMENT. HE'S A GREAT MOVER, TOO
KEVIN

THE UK NEEDS LEMAR – AN ARTIST WITH A GREAT VOICE TO SING MAINSTREAM BLACK POP MUSIC
CARRIE

SINGING TO WIN

SINGING TO WIN

Wednesday

It's the last full day in the Academy and the students are going through one final class with Kevin, who has become something of a guru to them all. "I'd like to take this opportunity to thank Kevin Adams for his hard work and dedication" announces Sinead, echoing the feelings of all the students. "I'm touched" he responds, "But even without your thanks: I got paid." We know he loves 'em all, really!

As an extra incentive to give it their all on Friday, the students visit the luxury flat in St John's Wood and are blown away that one of them will actually be living there soon. "It does scare the life out of me, like" confesses Sinead. "Did you think, 'this will be mine'?" asks Carrie, probingly. "There's a lot to live up to" is Sinead's thoughtful reply. In a teacher's meeting, Richard is concerned that the pressure they are under has made them all get a bit run-down. Carrie agrees, but reinforces that it's a combination of things getting to all of the students: "The reality of it coming to an end, the pressure of needing to win, the late nights…" The pressure isn't going to ease off too much after the final show, either, as nine additional dates have been added to the Fame Academy tour in Spring 2003 and the album is Number One in the compilation charts. Sinead is so excited at the news she smashes a Christmas bauble and shouts the unofficial Fame Academy motto "Damn it, damn it" as she clears the debris up.

Finally, each student gives their last ever speech in the lounge, with Lemar going first. "I have come a long way on this journey and learnt a lot of things about me. The whole Lionel Ritchie thing was amazing, " he tells the group. Sinead thanks everyone from the kitchen staff to the cameramen and is honest about her feelings as the final Showdown approaches: "I got in with the public vote, but I am not going to take it for granted. The things I have learnt in here have been priceless." Last but not least, David has his say: "I was sceptical at first, but I have learnt a lot more than I thought I would. Everything the tutors have taught me has enabled me to be a better singer. I think all three of us will do ourselves proud… cheers guys!"

Thursday

With just one day to go until the final, the rehearsals at Shepperton Studios are proving a tense, but enjoyable experience for the remaining three students. Despite the fact that it's freezing and they're all suffering from colds, they're in really upbeat moods. David is walking around wrapped in a technicolour fleecy blanket to try to keep warm, Lemar is bouncing around cheerfully, while Sinead – still managing to look gorgeous despite her sniffles – is sipping hot honey and lemon to help soothe her throat. "I'm feeling rotten!" she exclaims. "I hope I'm okay for tomorrow night. I'm so worried about my throat."

As if to torment them further, the super sleek Audi TT sports car the winner will be zooming around in is parked outside the studio for all to see. "Oh, it's gorgeous. I have to sing soooo well tomorrow!" David drools when he sees it, giving it a quick stroke. David is also stunned when Johnny Vegas – who's at Shepperton Studios shooting a new film – asks him for his autograph; apparently his "missus" is a big fan! "Oh my God, I'm such a big fan of his. I can't believe he asked me for my autograph!" laughs David in disbelief. Afterwards Johnny reveals that he's not letting his wife anywhere near the smiling Scot. "If my wife thinks I'm gonna bring her along tomorrow night she's got another thing coming, because I'm not gonna lose the love of my life to a Fame Academy student!" Up in the dressing room area, the three finalists rush to get their chow down as there's a string of TV crews poised to do interviews with them. The students join the teachers for lunch, but David is shunning a big meal in favour of some soup and: "some Irn Bru if you've got it!" (A Scot through and through!)

For once the teachers are making more noise than the students. As they all chat and laugh, Kevin sings 'Angels' and 'In the Midnght Hour' at the top of his voice. When lunch has been quaffed, it's time for the students to face the cameras and at 7pm, they're rounded up and taken back the Academy. The trio then pack their cases for the last time before bedtime.

With just one day to go until they discover their fate, we reckon tonight is going to be one hell of a long night for the talented trio…

Sing for Survival

AFTER TEN WEEKS, MANY TEARS, A FEW CHEEKY SNOGS AND A WHOLE LOT OF SINGING, THE FAME ACADEMY FINAL SHOWDOWN HAS FINALLY ARRIVED. THE NEXT FEW HOURS WILL CHANGE ONE LUCKY STUDENT'S LIFE FOREVER.

In The Orangery function room at Shepperton Studios, pre-show drinks are being enjoyed by the friends and family of the students and a host of celebrities including Dr Fox, TV presenters Linda Barker and Dale Winton, DJ Emma B, 'Eastenders' stars Nicholas Bailey and Adam Woodyatt, 'The Office' actor MacKenzie Crook and actress and presenter Jocie D'arby. Inside the studio the atmosphere is already electric. Sinead, David and Lemar come on and stand on the stage with huge smiles on their faces. They wave at the audience, friends and family and the ex-students and then look nervously at each other. The audience go wild and Cat and Patrick welcome everyone to the Fame Academy Final.

Cat gives each finalist a hug and kiss while Patrick introduces all the students and teachers. As Sinead will be singing first, Lemar and David walk to the side of the stage to wait their turn, and take the opportunity to embrace their former Academy mates.

After telling Cat "I'm ready!" Sinead strides up to the microphone and launches into 'Don't Speak'. Afterwards, Patrick asks Carrie if it was a winning performance. "It could be. It's down to the audience," is her diplomatic reply, while Jeremy declares: "I do think she has what it takes. She's a very strong willed young woman and has a wise head on young shoulders." It seems Sinead was pleased with how it went herself, saying: "It was grand!"

Lemar is next to perform and seems as laid back as ever. "Does nothing rattle Mr. Cool?" Cat asks him. Lemar replies that he is "quite nervous, but there's a lot of people on my side." After his rendition of 'Let's Stay Together' – during which he sparkles in a pair of £15,000 trousers – the teachers are full of praise. "There's no one in the Academy that can interpret a song like Lemar. That was fantastic," Carrie claims, while Jeremy adds: "He really knows how to work the audience". "I feel great now. One down, one to go!" Lemar laughs.

A terrified looking David prepares to perform. A group of girls in the audience shout: "We love you David!" and he rewards them with his trademark grin. Carrie says that she's pleased that he's got rid of his old bad singing habits, but causes controversy when she declares that he shouldn't sing with a Glasweigen accent. He manages to leave all his bad habits behind and whip the audience into a frenzy with his version of 'Don't Let The Sun Go Down On Me'. Patrick asks Richard who he thinks has the most potential to have a long term career and he chooses David. David is ecstatic about this long-awaited recognition: "It's about time, Richard. It's only taken ten weeks!"

It's time for the audience to vote for their favourite performance and when the votes are counted Sinead is the clear winner with 46%, David comes in second with 31%, while Lemar is third with 23%. The finalists are singing two songs on the first part of the show – one cover and one self-penned track – and Lemar is up next with 'Lullaby', the track he co-wrote with Ainslie. All the students sing along and Kevin's verdict is "It worked for me, but I'm not at home voting. So I hope it worked down the lens." David takes his place at a piano on stage and sings 'Living A Lie'. He gives an emotional performance and Pam is full of praise, saying: "He's been the most prolific songwriter in the Academy. He's matured over the last ten weeks." Finally it's Sinead's turn to showcase her track,' I Can't Break Down'. "I think it's a great song. I love it to bits. It's got that gutsy rock chick thing going on," says a smiling Pam of her performance.

There's some good news for all of the students when they are presented with a platinum disk for the Fame Academy album. Then it's decision time for the expelled students when Patrick grills some of them about who they want to win. "They're all absolutely fantastic, but I personally want David to win," Marli professes. Camilla picks Lemar as "his voice is amazing and he's got his own unique sound." Not surprisingly, Malachi's support goes to Sinead. "My vote has to go for the Irish lass!" Messages from famous Fame Academy fans are flashed up on the huge screens and Eammon Holmes and Adam Woodyatt are backing Sinead, Jono Coleman, Emma Forbes and Holly Valance want David to win, while Lemar has Hermione Norris, Kate Lawler, Blazin' Squad, Jeremy Edwards, Tina Hobley and Ja Rule rooting for him.

The phone lines are closed and shortly one of the final three students will be expelled, while the remaining two will battle if out in the second part of the show. While the votes are being counted up, Patrick takes the opportunity to chat to the students' relatives. Lemar's brother, Duraine, says "Lemar is the person who will give you a lifetime of sweet sensation!" Sinead's mum says that she's "coping the best" at being the mum of a superstar, while David's dad says: "He's talented, he's funny, and he's worked hard. By God he deserves to be in the final."

Over four million votes have been cast and as the students rise up from under the stage in a cloud of dry ice, the studio is deadly silent.The students walk down the stage and stand facing the front. Everyone anxiously waits for Cat to announce who will be the first student to leave the final showdown. After what seems like hours, she announces that David is the first student who will be going through to the head to head. Lemar and Sinead hug

him, Marli and Nigel go mad and his family jump up and down. Sinead and Lemar hold hands while they wait to find out who will continue to the final round. After a tense wait, it's announced that Sinead will go up against David, meaning that Lemar must say goodbye. He hugs Sinead while Lemar and Sinead's family embrace each other. Kevin runs on stage and hugs Lemar as Cat announces: "I've got a feeling it's not going to end here!" After a gracious round of compliments to all the tutors, Lemar walks off down the stage runway and into the waiting arms of his family.

Up in the BBC Choice studio, the ex-students are relaxing with a beer and there are huge cheers when Lemar enters the studio. During his interview with Danaan and Vanessa, Lemar is upbeat and no matter how much he's pressed, he won't admit whether he wants David or Sinead to win. He rounds off the show by singing an incredible version of Robbie Williams' 'Angels'. Afterwards he hugs his girlfriend, Charmaine, signalling that they are very much back together and she has forgiven him for his little indiscretion with Camilla. The second part of the show is about to start and everyone is firmly back in their seats in the main studio. Malachi goes over to talk to Sinead's family, then being the fair chap that he is, goes over to chat to David's mum and dad too. In the student zone, Chris is doing a dance routine and trying to encourage Nigel to join in, while the female students are grooving to Pink's 'Get The Party Started'.

David and Sinead come on stage in a glamorous costume change and Sinead admits to Patrick she is: "A bit nervous now. But I'm going to give it everything. That's all I can do." David is as cheery as ever, saying: "I just keep telling myself that the worst I can do is come second and that's not too shabby!" David kicks off the second part of the show by singing Everything But The Girl's 'I Don't Want To Talk About It'. Carrie is hugely impressed. "That was a really composed performance. He totally knows how to sell a ballad." Richard is equally enthusiastic, claiming: "The future looks good for David Sneddon, doesn't it? He'll be an artist to contend with worldwide." Cat comments to David on how proud his family look, "My mum looks like her head's about to explode!" he says jokingly.

It's Sinead's turn to sing to win and her chosen track is Rod Stewart's 'The First Cut Is The Deepest'. Malachi is up and clapping before she's even started and once again, Carrie is full of praise. "She's got a voice that kicks butt." She also comments that Sinead is very inspirational to women as she's not "Your skinny model type". "I'm delighted. I agree wholeheartedly!" Sinead grins, patting her stomach.

With just 15 minutes to go before the winner of Fame Academy is announced, Pat chats to Sinead and David's supporters again. David's mum – whose head is thankfully still intact – says "I'm so nervous! Just be yourself David. We're so proud of you and you deserve it." Sinead's dad shakes his head and says simply: "Thank God she's got this far." The final song of the night is Elton John's 'I Guess That's Why They Call It the Blues'. David performs the first half while Sinead sways along on the side of the stage, then she strolls down the runway and takes up the song. They finish by singing the final few lines together, their voices harmonising perfectly.

There are some kind words from their student friends afterwards with Malachi saying of Sinead: "She's been herself the whole way through the experience. Every Friday she's got up and performed like a star and tonight is no different. She deserves it." Family man Nigel then tells David: "Your songs are amazing. Keep it up. You're going to be a star."

The time has come for Sinead and David to discover who will be walking away with the incredible prize package that is sure to make one of them a superstar. After rising up dramatically from underneath the stage, both take their place in the spotlight and hold hands. An incredible 6.9 million votes have been cast and after what feels like the longest pause in history, it's announced that with 3.5 million of those votes, the winner is… David!

He looks absolutely astonished and falls to his knees and covers his face with his hands as fireworks go off around him. He gets to his feet again and his elated family run on and embrace him. David's girlfriend, Eleanor, leaps dramatically into his arms and Sinead hugs and congratulates him, before her mum runs on to give her a comforting hug. David jumps around and lets out a series of whoops before clenching his fists and looking into the audience and shouting: "Come oooooooon!" Before you know it all the students and teachers have joined him on stage. Everyone is running around hugging each other and Nigel and Chris hoist the victorious student up onto their shoulders while he punches the air in delight.

"I can't believe I've won!" David shouts ecstatically, looking close to tears. It's time for David's final Fame Academy performance and as he steps up to the mike to sing 'Living A Lie', he's so excited he's finding it hard to get the words out. He smiles his trademark smile and raises his eyebrows and in the blink of a competition, David Sneddon – Pop Star, is born. "This is my single," he shouts halfway through the track, shaking his head in disbelief. When he's finished performing he rejoins the throng on stage and as sparkling confetti rains down upon their heads, they all hold hands, hug and reflect on an incredible ten weeks. David tells everyone: "I never thought I'd win!" and then dedicates his award to Naomi, whom he replaced on the show nine weeks ago. He also shouts: "Thanks to my parents and teachers who supported me. This is for my girlfriend as well."

Sinead is taking her defeat incredibly gracefully and when asked if she's disappointed about not winning, she replies sincerely: "Do you know what? I enjoyed every single second. I couldn't have lost out to a better person." The cameras stop rolling and the first ever Fame Academy term comes to a close. But the night isn't over yet for a certain Scottish star.

As David leaves the studio and walks along the Fame Academy red carpet he's greeted by the flashing bulbs of paparazzi cameras and excited autograph hunters, before being whisked off to the aftershow party. This is what the pop star lifestyle is all about and he had better get used to it!

interview
Lemar

FANTASTIC FINALIST LEMAR HAS NO REGRETS
ABOUT HIS TIME IN FAME ACADEMY.
ALTHOUGH THERE IS ONE THING HE WISHES
EVERYONE HADN'T SEEN...

How was the Final Live Showdown experience for you?
It was such a good night. Mad, but good.

Were you nervous before the show?
Yes, I think that was the first show I was nervous about, but once I sang the nerves went. I was prepared for whatever happened. David and Sinead are very popular people and I hadn't won a public vote, so I was a bit of an underdog. But I enjoyed myself.

How did you feel when you found out you hadn't won?
I saw it coming, to be honest. When it was just Sinead and I on stage I said to her: "If you go through, make sure you do well." I wasn't disappointed at all because I was really happy that I'd got to the last three and had so many opportunities.

Was it lovely seeing your friends and family afterwards?
It was so lovely. We got to hug and have a quick chat.

So how is life back in the real world?
It's fine. I've had some time off to spend with my family, which has been great. I saw my brother's baby yesterday, which was so lovely. It's weird that people know who I am so I'm still getting used to people recognising me, but it's very, very, very exciting.

Have you spoken to David since you've been out?
No. Things are manic for him, so I want to leave it a couple of days and then see what he's up to. I wish him the best of luck and I'll have a chat with him soon.

Have you got any regrets about Fame Academy?
Not a single one. It's been great and my life's changed, hopefully for the better. It's so weird having had a taste of life outside the Academy. I would never, ever, ever in my wildest dreams have imagined my life would go like this. I've learnt loads and had some experiences I don't think I'll ever have in my life again.

What were your best and worst bits?
The best was duetting with Lionel Ritchie. That was such a highlight. The worst bits were every Saturday after you'd seen your family and friends on a Friday and not been able to speak to them. It's so hard. And there was always a lull after the show. It wasn't much fun.

Was Fame Academy what you expected?
It's much better than I expected. I thought it would be a show that I could go on and get some publicity, then come out and try and get a deal or something. But it's actually been a massive learning experience. I've learnt loads about myself, about my voice, about the other people in the show. I've learnt so, so much.

Did you ever think you'd get as far as you have?
No. When I first went in I said to myself that

if I could make it to the fourth week I would be happy. When the tenth week came and I was still in there, it was wicked.

Who did you think would win when you first went into the Academy?

Initially I thought Chris, Camilla and Marli would be up there, because I thought they were typically what people might want. But as time went on I thought Ainslie and Sinead had a good chance. By about the sixth week, I thought I may have a chance myself!

We have to ask about your snog with Camilla...

Oh. It was just... you're in there a long time, everyone's friends and she was a really good friend to me initially. Then she went, obviously, but when she came back to the reunion... I had quite a bit of champagne and we're just really good friends and we crossed the mark.

Do you regret it?

It's one of those things. I spoke to Jeremy at the time and he was like: "You don't want to worry about it, it's the past."

That phone call with Charmaine after it happened must have been incredibly hard for you both?

I knew everyone was watching, so it was awful.

Are things okay with you and Charmaine now?

It's fine. A kiss doesn't end a seven year relationship. She was upset with me, but she's there for me. I've been forgiven. I'm very lucky.

Ainslie described you as a 'cheap date' when it comes to booze. Are you not much a drinker?

No, I'm not. I'm a Malibu and coke or pineapple guy and everyone laughs at me. Drinking is something I'll have to learn. That's why Ainslie would have been so good if he'd won Fame Academy – he's a good rock'n'roll drinker!

Was it horrible when you were ill and were put in solitary confinement?

Actually, that was a nice opportunity to rest! The worst thing you could have in the show was a cold, so I knew I had to relax. And I was so pleased it cleared up in time for me to perform on the Live Showdown. I was lucky that that week the show was on the Sunday. If it hadn't been, I wouldn't have been able to perform properly.

You appeared to be a big fan of sleeping in the Academy...

That was taken out of context! I would wake up and do a three hour workout with Kevin, then I'd have a shower and after that your body's ready to have a fifteen minute nap. I didn't force myself to sleep. I'd just sit down on the couch and... zzzzzz. Then all of a sudden people started saying I was lazy. It's not true!

But you are pretty laid back and didn't always seem like you were gunning for the prize. How much did you want to win?

I really, really, really wanted to win. It would have been the icing on the cake. But I'm so happy with what I've achieved so for me it was a win/win situation.

Who were your closest mates in the Academy?

At first it was Camilla and Nigel was a kind of constant mate. As time went on, I got close to Malachi and Ainslie and of course, in the last week I got close to David and Sinead. But they were all good characters in there. I was closer to some people than others, but I got on with them all.

Was it weird when it was just the three of you in the last week?

Yeah. We were lucky we were kept so busy because the time we had to ourselves was so

quiet. Nothing really seemed to happen when we were left to do what we wanted. One person would be in the toilet, one would be working and I would be... asleep!

You must have been really pleased that you escaped probation until week nine?
Yes. I was so lucky probation came when it did because the voting was so close. I could have been out of there. I'm so glad I didn't have to face probation any other time apart from that. Once was bad enough.

How did you find the voting process?
It's so difficult. In the beginning I kept thinking: "Oh my god, I'm ending someone's life!" It was terrible. But about halfway through the series I got close to people and we all knew then that nothing was done maliciously. The Malachi or Ainslie decision was the hardest for me to make. It was not nice.

You had a record deal before which fell through. Did you ever feel like totally giving up on music?
Definitely. I tried to release a single before but the record company wasn't really behind me and it didn't work out. So I went back to working in Natwest Bank. While I was there I thought: "The music's just not working." so I applied to University to do computer programming and I got a place. Then I saw an advert for Fame Academy and I decided to give it a go. It was an opportunity to show me and my raw edge – and I was accepted and made it to the final!

You supported Destiny's Child when you had your record deal, didn't you?
I did. They played The Hippodrome and I managed to get on the bill. I met them briefly and I performed just before them. It was cool.

How did you get on with the Academy teachers?
They were great. I think they genuinely made their comments with your benefit in mind. Of course, it was hard if someone criticised you on a Friday night when you'd just given your all, but they were there to push us in the right direction. I appreciate everything they've done. Pam is brilliant, Jo is an amazingly talented lady and we know that Carrie and Kevin are great. Kevin's mad. I think if he hadn't been there in the last week it wouldn't have been anywhere near as much fun.

What about Richard – you had a bit of an argument when he described your performance of 'Yesterday' as uninspiring, didn't you?
Richard is a great bloke and I wasn't offended by what he said. I just think if he's in the position he's in and he's saying things like that then he should give me a reason. I wanted to know the reason why he didn't like it so I could improve. I wanted to have my say and tell him how I was feeling. I believe in credit where credit's due. I listened to the teachers all the time, but I also wanted reasons for their remarks, which I think is fair.

What are you planning to do now you've left Fame Academy?
I'd really like to do some music and record an album. So we'll see if there are any deals on the table and take it from there. I think it's going to be an interesting time.

Outspoken
Fame Academy

THE FAME ACADEMY STUDENTS AND TEACHERS TELL IT LIKE IT IS IN SOME OF THE BEST QUOTES FROM THE SERIES.

"The only place that success comes before work is in the dictionary."
Right on, Carrie

"I feel like I'm on a girlie holiday!"
Not for long, Pippa

"We want to get down to work if you don't mind. What do you think this is? A holiday camp?"
Are you listening, Pippa?

"I know it's pants, but we're writing pop songs to please the masses. Music for morons."
Charming, Ainslie!

"He makes me giggle and he's cute to look at!"
Which is why Marli would like to be stranded on a desert island with Ainslie

"Time is money and I don't come cheap."
And Kevin is worth every penny

"You make it as a star, then you misbehave – not the other way round."
Jeremy wishes Ainslie would behave

"You know when Lemar sings and you think 'What the hell am I doing in this place?'"
Nigel thinks his Academy-mate is Lemar-vellous

"This changes everything. To find a good-looking person who can sing is so difficult. To find a good-looking writer-musician, you go from being average to being the full package."
Carrie is amazed to discover David's hidden depths

"The sex is just oozing out of you!"
We think Malachi likes you, Sinead!

"Artists should be free. They shouldn't be disciplined. You speak to John Lennon or Tim Booth or Morrissey – people who actually deserve some respect and they are not disciplined."
Neither, it seems, is Ainslie

"I feel it should be a show about musicians and talent, not about people pretending to be in some little school. I think that's pathetic."
We heard you the first time, Ainslie!

"Will I have to drink wine and champagne or can I drink lager and black?"
She's a classy bird, that Katie

"Malachi, everyone thinks you and me should get it on!"
Oh, it won't be long, Sinead!

"Damn it! Damn it!"
Do you think David minded missing out on seeing The Doves?

Top Ten Morning Songs

These are our favourite tunes to wake the sleepy students each morning. Wonder if they got the joke at the time?

1 ▸ Winner Takes All, Abba
2 ▸ Morning Has Broken
3 ▸ When Will I Be Famous, Bros,
4 ▸ I Gotta Get Thru This, Daniel Bedingfield
5 ▸ Survivor, Destiny's Child
6 ▸ When The Going Gets Tough, Billy Ocean
7 ▸ Things Can Only Get Better, D:Ream
8 ▸ Reach, S Club 7
9 ▸ Livin' On a Prayer, Bon Jovi
10 ▸ Always On Time, Ja Rule

BEAUTIFUL SONGBIRD, SINEAD MAY HAVE LOST OUT TO DAVID IN THE FAME ACADEMY FINAL, BUT IT CERTAINLY WON'T BE THE LAST WE'LL HEAR OF HER.

How was the Fame Academy Final for you?

It was fantastic. I was really nervous and a bit shaky, but I just went for it and enjoyed it so much. The rehearsals were terrible because I was just so nervous. But they always say 'bad rehearsal, good show', so I was keeping my fingers crossed.

How did you feel when you realised David had won?

I was grand with it. I think I did so well to get where I did and I'm really happy for David. I am genuinely delighted for him, I think he deserves it. Best of luck to him. I'm proud of myself anyway. I was proud to be in the last four and to get into the final and sing my own song was the most important thing for me.

How did you feel when you were waiting to hear the result?

That was the moment I was most shaky. I could see my mum and dad were shaking as well. It seemed like such a long wait and David and I were just desperate to hear.

Was it great to see your friends and family again after the show?

Oh yes. It was great to have a good chat instead of three minute phone calls. It's been brilliant seeing everyone again.

How is life outside the Academy?

Everything's been really cool. It's been fantastic having some time to relax and sleep as much as I want! It was weird at first, but

I've adjusted really quickly. I thought I'd be looking for my mike and all that, but I haven't and I'm not missing the cameras at all.

How was life inside Fame Academy for you?

It was very mixed. There were ups and there were downs, but it was mostly ups for me. The homesickness kicked in a bit now and then, but generally it's been a great experience.

What were the best and worst parts?

The best were getting up there on a Friday night and performing. And of course the times when I got drunk and fell off treadmills and stuff! The whole thing was brilliant. I got to know people better and it was even more fun as the weeks went on. The worst bit was the homesickness. But I tried not to let it bother me.

What did you miss?

Friends and family, especially my wee brother. And we've got a new puppy as well. It's a terrier called Tara, and I haven't seen it yet. Apparently it s**ts round the house all the time! I miss my other wee dog, Chickenpie-facefeatures, as well. She's 12 – I got her for my tenth birthday – and she loves me. I also missed my phone. I rely on that thing. When I was at Uni I spoke to my mum twice a day. I'm not a real mummy's girl, but me and me ma have good old chats and I missed that.

What were the best and worst criticisms you got from the teachers?

The best was when they said I had the ability to

do an album. And when I got Grade A they said my voice had improved so much. The worst things were when they said I didn't do as well as others. I never got any criticism from Kevin, but I don't think my dancing was up to standard. I just got on and enjoyed it.

How was it being the only girl left in the last week?

It wasn't really any different. I always try to get on with people the best I can and I kept them boys in check. I could handle them. I took no s**t off them!

Who were you closest to?

Probably Malachi. Me and him got on really well. I really hit it off with Pippa too.

About you and Malachi... What's the situation?

Nothing, really. It was a bit of laugh and we're good friends. I think the world of him, he's lovely. Why the hell not snog? We're both single and we'd had a few glasses of champagne. Sometimes a girl just needs a good old snog.

Do you mind that everyone saw it?

I was drunk and thinking the cameras couldn't see us because it was dark. But at the same time I didn't care if they saw us. It just happened. It wasn't planned.

Was there anything you wish the cameras hadn't seen?

One time I was getting changed and when I took off my trousers a camera was looking right at me; me arse was there and I was wearing a thong. I turned round and sat on the bed so the camera couldn't see me and went: "F**k off!" I felt really uncomfortable with the cameras in the bedrooms when I was undressing and stuff. I'd just jump into the wardrobe!

Did being filmed 24 hours a day drive you mad?

You got used to it. But when it was just the three of us, every time we moved you could hear the whirring following you. That was a bit weird.

What do you think about the other snogs that happened inside the Academy?

Jeremy and Marli's snog – why not? I have no problem with it. Chris and Marli's snog was just a dare and Camilla and Lemar? I don't know about that one. He regrets it. It was just a drunken thing that happened. I know he thinks Camilla is great as a friend, but he thinks the world of his girlfriend. Mine and Malachi's snog was the best I think. I think the world of him.

Malachi said he was a bit disappointed the kiss was so short!

What's wrong with boys? I instigated the snog and he's taking all the credit! It has to be taken lightly, though. Everyone's asking me what's going to happen now and it's a bit of pressure because, who knows?

Which of the Fame Academy classes did you enjoy the most?

I enjoyed all of them, but probably songwriting the most. I didn't write as much as I should have done, though. I found it really intimidating with the cameras being there. You're coming out with personal, intimate stuff and it might look a bit naff to other people. It's a very private thing for me to do and I'll do more writing now I'm out of the Academy.

How did you get on with the teachers?

They were grand. If ever I needed to stick up for myself, I did. The only time I really got told off was when I took a trip down the stage when I was performing 'Ironic' on the Live Showdown.

What made you do that?

About ten minutes before I went on stage I was in floods of tears. My throat was hurting and half an hour before I was going on stage my clothes were being changed. And you know when you just want to chill out? It was the first time everything annoyed me, so I got on the stage and I thought: "I can either stay in this mood, or I can go out there and give a good performance and enjoy it." I think I gave a good performance considering the mood I was in! Fair enough, I should have stayed where I should have been, but I felt that I needed to give myself a lift of some sort. I didn't regret it afterwards.

What are the most important things you learnt?

A lot of stuff about myself personally. In one of the first PDP sessions people said they thought I was quiet, yet I've always thought myself to be a very sociable person, so it was kind of weird how people perceived me. I learnt a lot about my abilities. I never thought I'd be able to do a dance routine. Even though I didn't do it very well, I still managed to pull it together on some of the weeks.

How was it meeting all the Masterclass celebs and duetting with Ronan Keating?

Ronan was amazing and Lionel Ritchie was fantastic. He gave us really good advice. Shania Twain and Mariah Carey were really friendly as well. I would never have imagined three months ago that I would be meeting them. It's so surreal and it's only when you come out of the Academy and people ask you about things that you realise what you've done.

Did you mind when Ainslie borrowed your pants that time?

I didn't care, but I want to see a video of him wearing them! He said he had no pants and I said he could wear my granny pants, so he did. I really can't wait to see it.

Which of your fellow students do you think you'll stay in touch with?

Definitely Malachi because he lives in Ireland as well, and probably all of the last few. I never really got to know Chris or Ashley that well and Camilla left quite early, but I would like to stay in touch with as many people as possible. It won't be easy because we all live all over the place, but I've promised Pippa I'll go and have a night out in Hull!

Do you feel like your life has changed forever?

It has, but it's up to me how I want to deal with it. I don't think I've changed personally. I don't want or need to change. I come from a very small town and everyone knows me for who I am. I'm chilled out, and my family would kick my arse if I changed at all!

Has it sunk in yet that you've left the Academy?

No, it feels so strange. I haven't really had time to reflect on it yet. People keep saying to me: "Do you remember when you did this and that." so I think it will really hit me when I go home and sit down and watch the videos.

What are your plans for the future?

I'm still in discussions with people, but hopefully I'll have a single out next year. Hopefully an album as well. I've got the hunger and the drive to do it. I want to write tunes and get them out and bring something new to the charts.

Interview
David

WE HAVE A WINNER! GREAT SCOT DAVID SNEDDON HAS
SCOOPED THE BIGGEST PRIZE IN TV HISTORY AND HIS LIFE
WILL NEVER BE THE SAME. WE GET THE FEELING HE'S
REALLY QUITE EXCITED ABOUT IT ALL!

Congratulations on winning! How are you feeling?

It's incredible. It's all kind of passing in a blur at the moment. More than anything, I'm looking forward to getting home for a couple of weeks to reflect on everything I've done. It's so manic, but I'm really, really enjoying it.

Do you feel like a pop star yet?

A little bit. I've been doing lots of interviews and I'm going into the recording studio today which I think will make everything feel real. At the moment it feels like when I go back home for Christmas it will all be over, but it's only just begun. I've just realised I can't do my Christmas shopping in Glasgow because it will be mad for me. I'm going to have to adjust to this new kind of lifestyle for however long it lasts.

Can you describe how you felt the moment you discovered you had won?

The whole thing is a blur, but I remember that when Patrick Kielty said "David" everything went on fire! I remember how shocked I was and then these flames shot up from the front of the stage. I was so happy that I'd forgotten that I had to go and sing my song again. I can't put into words how I felt. I was totally ecstatic and I couldn't believe that I'd actually managed to win.

Especially as you were the latecomer...

Yes, it's so weird to think that if Naomi hadn't lost her voice, there would have been another winner on this show, because I wouldn't have been there. That's the incredible thing. It just shows you that at the auditions there must have been hundreds of people like me who were incredibly talented but missed out. The audition process is so hard, there will be people that didn't get their chance. I was so fortunate. I don't think that I was the best by a long shot, but I think I deserved it because of the hard work I put in. We all worked so hard. Now that I've won, I can sit back and appreciate everything I've been through and it will start to become real.

Are you excited about recording an album?

Oh yes! I've got tons of songs ready. Hundreds. But because I've had this experience I kind of want to write some new ones. I'm probably going to write a few over Christmas, even though I'm supposed to be relaxing. I just really want to get started. I've had more life experiences in the last twelve weeks than I've had in my whole life and it's all going to add to my songwriting.

Has it sunk in that you're releasing a single soon?

That's obviously the major thing for me. I can't believe it. It feels like I've known 'Living A Lie' all my life because I wrote it when I was 17. It's a song that's always been quite special to me, so to have it released as a single is the best part of my prize.

How did you celebrate your win after the show?

There was an aftershow party, but I spent most of the night talking to all the executives and the like. I was taken from one place to another and had to do interviews. I also had to get up at half five the next morning to do 'The Saturday Show', so I think the celebrations will really start when I get home. I'm very happy, so I don't feel like I've missed out on any celebrations.

When are you moving into the flat?
This week is so busy with TV shows and interviews that I'm staying in hotels. Then I'm going back to Scotland for a couple of weeks, then I'll come down and settle into my flat. I can move in whenever I want, but I want to wait until the madness dies down a little bit.

Are you planning to have some wild parties there?
Oh yes, absolutely! I have to have a flat-warming. We said that whoever won Fame Academy had to have a party in the flat for all the students.

Have you driven the car yet?
No, I haven't even sat in it yet! But I've seen it and it's gorgeous. I'm getting it in a couple of days and I plan to drive home to Scotland in it.

Of course, you've got a cameo in a film to come as well. Do you know which film it's going to be?
No. I've heard a few rumours that it's 'Harry Potter', but I don't know. I've yet to find out. But that's great because it's means I've got more surprises to come. This next year is going to be tremendous for me.

When are you jetting off to the Caribbean for your holiday?
I'm not sure, but I'm so looking forward to it. I forgot I've got tickets to the FA Cup Final as well. I'm football daft so that's such a major prize for me. There's so much happening, it's going to be incredible.

You've waited so long for all this. Has it been worth the wait?
Yes. It feels as if all my hard work over the past few years has built up to this moment. It's made everything I've done in the past seem worthwhile. The stupid little things I've done to try to get money, the fact I've been really down about not having a real job or a record contract; it all makes me appreciate what I've got now.

How are you going to cope being so far away from your friends, family and girlfriend Eleanor?
My friends and family are all very down to earth. The worst thing about being in the Academy was being completely cut off, whereas now I've got my phone and they can visit me and I can visit them. I've got some friends in London as well, so it's not as if I've run away and I'm never going to see anyone again. And Eleanor's only got a few months left of her degree and then she's talking about coming down to London.

Have you been recognised a lot since you've been out?
All the time. A photographer wanted to take a picture of me outside this morning and people were stopping their cars and saying congratulations.

Were you shocked when you got your second chance to go in to the Fame Academy after losing out to Sinead in the first show?
Yes. I was lying on my bed on a Sunday morning with a slight hangover and I got a phone call at about eleven o'clock. They were straight to the point and said: "Hi, we've got a problem with one of the students and we would like you to come into the Academy." I was very wary because I'd watched the first week's show and it wasn't very good, so I'd had a week to reflect on it. The week I'd been back in Glasgow I'd been singing in a band and I'd had some

interest from a couple of record companies, so I was debating whether or not to go in.

What made you decide to go for it?
I chatted to my parents and my girlfriend and I was at that stage in my life where I'd decided this could be my last chance at music. I decided that if I went into the Academy and worked hard and tried my best, something would happen.

Did you expect to get into the final?
No. I hadn't even considered it.

When did you think you would be going out?
I didn't think about getting further than a couple of weeks. The first night I was on probation I'd only been in the Academy for six or seven days so I expected to go straight out. Winning the public vote was lovely, especially as I think I had about 54% of the votes. From there on I built on my strengths and kept working hard. I was making friends and it was starting to feel good. I'm very positive so I just kept working hard and smiling and suddenly I found myself in the final. Each week I didn't expect to get anywhere, so to get to the final...

You were the outsider at first. But who was and who wasn't welcoming to you?
You know what I'm going to say here! Malachi was really open to me. The first day I went in he showed me around. He's probably the only person who was friends with everyone. He's such a nice guy. From the first night I knew Nigel and I would get on and Marli sort of took me in. Katie is also a wee star - I love her to death - and Lemar is a good mate. But for the first couple of weeks, Ainslie didn't want to know me at all. That's because I replaced Naomi who was a very good friend of his. He was also a bit wary about another young Scottish guy coming in.

Did that annoy you?
A bit, but the good thing about Ainslie, that made me gain a little respect for him, is that he tells you how it is. For the first two weeks it was uneasy between us, but after a fortnight that cleared up and the two of us suddenly became good mates. But the perception that we didn't get on still existed outside the Academy and people kept on about it. It was great when it came to a head on the Live Showdown and he and I said it was a load of rubbish.

Everyone thought you might get together with Katie...
I have a girlfriend who I'm really happy with and certainly at the moment there's not going to be anyone that can turn my head from her. She's perfect for me. There was a little bit of a flirty relationship with me and Katie just because I'm a guy and she's a girl, but Katie was like a little sister to me. I really bonded with her because we were always jumping about and it was really good fun. We clicked as friends and it's purely platonic. I'm friends with her in the same way I am with Nigel and no one's asking me if I fancied him!

Did you?
No!

You were really smiley throughout the show, but you did cry when Nigel left and you got put on probation the same night...
They were spin-offs of the main problem, which was homesickness. Fame Academy was the first time I'd been away from home for any length of time. You didn't have your phone, people couldn't come and visit and you could see your family on a Friday night, but you couldn't go and talk to them. It was almost like a form of torture. Whenever I was feeling down or low it was based on homesickness.

Why do you think Nigel going hit you so hard?

Nigel was my best mate in there. I was feeling so miserable about missing home and Nigel was the only person at that stage that I could sit and talk to about it. Everything got on top of me and I couldn't pull myself out of it.

Did being on probation bother you?

To be honest, I quite enjoyed the experience. There's something nice about getting up there and proving yourself because there are people who don't think you can do it.

Was there any time when you wanted to leave the Academy?

No. There were times when I said I hated it and wanted to get out, but every day there was something that made me laugh and made me glad I was there, which kept me going. There was no way I would have walked out.

Did you worry about people seeing you when you played the piano naked?

Not really. I think if I'd worried about it I wouldn't have done it. I knew the BBC wouldn't show everything, so it was good fun. I was still fairly new at that time so I just thought: "What the hell?!'"

Who did you think was going to win when you first went into the Academy?

It was between Lemar and Marli.

Is there anyone you think went too soon?

Camilla. I think if she'd got herself together earlier on in the series she might have gone on to do better things. In rehearsals she always sounded a lot better then she did on the show. I think there were a lot of nerves there.

Which of your performances was your favourite?

Singing 'Living A Lie', which was my own song.

I'd always wanted to do that since I was a kid, so it was like realising some kind of dream. It was brilliant.

Did it frustrate you that you were accused of being too boy band?

It didn't really bother me because I've had it all my life. The day after the comment was made, I played Carrie one of my songs and everything changed. I think when I record some more songs, people will stop saying things like that.

What's your opinion on the Fame Academy snogs?

The Lemar and Camilla one is so hard. Lemar really regrets it. He was drunk and Camilla is quite flirty. You don't make any excuses for it, but I spoke to him the morning after and I know how bad he felt. He was gutted and felt stupid. I'm not 100% sure what happened with Jeremy and Marli, we only heard bits and pieces. I think they were all just a bit of fun, to be honest.

How would you sum up your Fame Academy experience?

It's been mind-blowing. I'm well aware that I'm going to have to take some knocks along the way, but whatever happens, Fame Academy has been the best thing I've ever done in my life.

THE WINNER OF FAME ACADEMY

DAVID SNEDDON